stop buying mutual funds

Easy Ways to Beat the Pros Investing on Your Own

MARK J. HEINZL

JOHN WILEY & SONS CANADA, LTD

Toronto • New York • Chichester • Weinheim • Brisbane • Singapore

John Wiley & Sons Canada Limited
22 Worcester Road
Etobicoke, Ontario
M9W1L1

Canadian Cataloguing in Publication Data

Heinzl, J. Mark, 1967-
    Stop buying mutual funds: easy ways to beat the pros investing on your own
Includes index.

ISBN 0-471-64316-5

1. Stocks. 2. Bonds. 3. Mutual funds. I. Title.

HG4521.H44 1998   332.63'2   C98-932036-7

Production Credits
Cover & text design: Interrobang Graphic Design Inc.
Printer: Tri-Graphic Printing

Printed in Canada
10 9 8 7 6 5 4 3 2

To my Mom and Dad

Contents

Preface

One day in 1996 I was sitting in a fancy boardroom of a law firm in one of Toronto's office towers. Some stakeholders of the mutual fund company Altamira Management Ltd. had summoned members of the business news media to a meeting. They wanted to explain why they were taking legal action to block a takeover offer by Manufacturers Life Insurance Co. The offer valued Altamira at about $660 million. Meanwhile, Altamira's flagship Canadian equity mutual fund was significantly underperforming Canada's main stock index in 1996, just as it would the following year. The fund was very popular among Canadians because it had outperformed the index for several consecutive years prior to 1996.

As the stakeholders and lawyers droned on, my mind started to wander. Why all the fuss over a mutual fund company? Why would anyone pay so much for Altamira, a relatively new, "no-load" fund company? Then it occurred to me that the Altamira Equity fund had more than $2.5 billion of Canadians' money invested around that time, and was charging its investors more than 2.2 % of their money in fees and costs every year, no matter how well (or badly) it performed. In 1996, the Altamira Equity fund collected a total of $59.96 million in management fees and other expenses from its investors. In 1997, that figure was $58.95 million. That was just one of Altamira's twenty-odd mutual funds.

No wonder there was a fight for Altamira, I thought. A major stake was later sold to a U.S. firm in a transaction which valued the company at about $784 million.

Since then I've put a lot of thought into the world of investing and the way people behave with money. I marvel at the billions of dollars that change hands in the capital markets every day, and at the pinstriped money managers all trying to beat the market averages. Small investors hand over their hard-earned savings to these so-called "experts" in the hopes of seeing strong investment returns. It reminds me of the crowds that fill the casinos, racetracks, and lottery booths, all seeking the big score that never seems to happen. It struck me that while all this money flies back and forth, the middlemen must be making a killing. And they are.

Many of Canada's nouveau riche in the 1990s, in fact, are those who were fortunate enough to own a stake in the companies that sell and operate the mutual funds, rather than a stake in the mutual funds themselves. Several of the people who own a piece of the big fund companies are multimillionaires, even as the fund investors often receive substantially below-average returns on their money.

There's no law against anyone making a bundle of money on the people who invest in mutual funds. And Canada's mutual fund industry has done well to show Canadians that investing beyond GICs offers much greater potential rewards. If it weren't for the mutual funds drawing billions of dollars of new money into the market, stocks wouldn't have surged the way they have in the 1990s.

But there appears to be a continued lack of understanding among Canadians about how much they're paying to invest, and the effects that fees have on their returns. Many of the people who comment, advise, and write books about mutual funds give a biased view of investing since they're often aligned with the mutual fund industry or with specific funds. Though the issue of mutual fund fees has emerged in the major news media in the past year or so, much of the commentary tends to come to the same ho-hum conclusion: that investors should be mindful of fund fees but stick with mutual funds anyway.

In fact, it's easy for anyone to invest without mutual funds and keep fees to a bare minimum. This book will show you, step-by-step and in plain English, how to build a winning portfolio. It's not rocket science, and your do-it-yourself portfolio will have all the diversity, security, and growth potential that the big fund companies crow about.

So the following is a little light reading about Canadian mutual funds and their performance in recent years, plus some ideas for investors who want to avoid harmful mutual fund charges and manage their own money. The book was inspired partly by friends and acquaintances who related stories about poor mutual fund returns, high fees, and advisors who don't tell the whole story about investing. It was also inspired, though perhaps unknowingly, by the several people I've met who work in the mutual fund industry and invest on their own rather than through funds! Finally, I was also inspired by my grandmother, who could have used a book like this one. She lost most of her life savings because of bad advice from a so-called "professional."

Acknowledgements

I'd like to thank the following people for their input and assistance in the development of this book: Tony DiSilvestro, Geoff Hancock, John Heinzl, Rich Heinzl, Jim Lane, Edward Trapunski, Maria Yang, and the folks at John Wiley & Sons Canada Ltd, Dow Jones Canada, and *The Wall Street Journal*. Many more friends and acquaintances also offered valuable advice.

I'd also like to thank my parents Jane and Rudy for their wise counsel, and my dear wife, Paula, a great source of inspiration and of answers to a million crazy questions.

The Top Ten Reasons Why
You Shouldn't Buy Mutual Funds

1. The returns of most mutual funds fail to keep up with the market averages.

2. Mutual funds have Management Expense Ratios (MERs) ranging from about 0.5% to 3% of assets per year, and these expenses significantly reduce your returns over the long term.

3. Loads as high as 5% further reduce your returns, and aren't reflected in the posted returns of mutual funds.

4. Mutual funds can make you pay capital-gains taxes on other investors' capital gains. And most mutual funds make frequent distributions of capital gains, which create unwanted tax payments that reduce returns.

5. Index mutual funds substantially lag the index, whereas low-fee index-tracking stocks do a much better job.

6. Buying your own stocks and bonds is far more economical than buying mutual funds. It's also easy, fun, educational, and doesn't require a big time commitment or special knowledge of business.

7. Discount brokers are lowering the cost of investing, offering more services, and provide thorough monthly financial statements.

8. Mutual fund investments are out of your control and in some cases may conflict with your ethical standards.

9. Many financial advisors and stockbrokers will only sell you investments that generate a commission for them, and not the best returns for you.

10. You'll make your broker or investment advisor rich before you are.

A Hard Look at Mutual Funds

Everybody knows someone with the "do-it-yourself" approach to life. Think of the guy who repairs his car and house on his own, the woman who cuts her children's hair, the neighbours who built their backyard deck and renovated the basement by themselves. These resourceful people like to learn how things work, and they enjoy a challenge. They also save buckets full of money as they go through life!

Investing is no different. There's no reason why you can't buy stocks, bonds, and other investments on your own, through a discount broker, instead of through mutual funds, full-service brokers, or investment advisors. Your investments will have a big advantage over mutual funds and most stockbrokers' picks for one simple reason: lower fees.

When it comes to investing, the amount you're paying in fees is about the only thing you can control. You can't predict changes in stock prices, interest rates, or a stock's dividend payouts. But you can keep investment fees to a bare minimum.

This book will show you why investing on your own is the best route for all types of investors, and it will show you how to do it simply. You don't have to become an expert on stocks and bonds, and investing on your own can take as little or as much time as you want to put into it. Today, a growing number of low-cost alternatives to mutual funds make do-it-yourself investing a snap.

Consider this:

If a man approached you in the supermarket one day and offered to select your food items for you for a mere 2% of your grocery bill, what would you tell him? Most of us would suggest he go fly a kite.

If you were driving along looking for gasoline and saw that Bill's Gas 'n Go was charging 61 cents a litre while Randy's Gas Rite next door charged 57 cents, where would you pull in? It would be Randy's for most people.

Suppose you saw a sweater you wanted selling for $45 at The Clothing Guy and the exact same sweater at Crazy Al's selling for $39. Where would you buy the sweater? Al may be crazy, but he sells a lot more sweaters than the Guy.

The answers to these shopping questions are painfully obvious to most of us. But when it comes to saving and investing, many Canadians are terrible shoppers. That's because they're paying high fees to invest in mutual funds and make other investments, without considering the far cheaper alternative of do-it-yourself investing.

Creating your own quality, low-risk investment portfolio is easy to do; it costs far less; it's fun and educational, and it has a big advantage over mutual funds.

Canadians have been complaining about banks and their service charges for years, but few complain about high mutual fund fees. This is odd, because mutual fund charges are much higher than bank service charges for most people. Our bank service charges tend to run in the tens of dollars per year, while the typical fund investor pays several hundred dollars annually in mutual fund charges. One explanation for the lack of complaints about mutual fund charges could be that we are happy to pay substantial sums for the convenience of mutual fund investing. A more likely explanation, however, is that too many Canadians are unaware of the fees they're paying to invest. A 1997 study, in fact, showed that more than half of Canada's mutual fund investors aren't aware that they pay any annual fees whatsoever! All mutual funds charge their investors annual fees, whether you know it or not.

The Canadian mutual fund industry is exploding. Assets have ballooned from less than $50 billion in 1991 to more than $300 billion in early 1998, and they are likely to double again in a few years. Canadians have been fleeing safe, but low-yielding, Guaranteed Investment Certificates and Canada Savings Bonds to invest in mutual funds like never before. This amazing trend has a strong correlation with the rise in the stock market over the last several years.

Saving and investing are becoming more important every year for Canadians. Governments are constantly cutting services and offloading more financial responsibilities, such as saving for retirement, to the public. Few expect the Canada Pension Plan will provide anything near the amount of income most of us will need for retirement. That's why it's so important that we get the most from our investments. But a close examination of mutual fund returns over the past 10 years shows clearly that many investments aren't delivering.

	TSE 300	Stock Funds
One year	15.0%	13.2%
Five years	17.5%	15.1%
Ten years	11.0%	10.2%

Of the 196 Canadian equity mutual funds tracked by *The Globe and Mail* in 1997, only 76 were able to beat the return of 15% posted by the Toronto Stock Exchange 300 index. The average equity mutual fund return was 13.2% and the median return was 13.5%. (The median means there were an equal number of funds with better and worse performance than 13.5%.)

For the five years to Dec. 31, 1997, the average annual Canadian equity mutual fund return was 15.1%, the median fund return was 14.6%, and the comparable TSE 300 return was 17.5%. And for the 10 years to Dec. 31, 1997, the average annual mutual fund return was 10.2%, the median return was 10.0%, and the TSE 300 return was 11.0%.

Mutual funds that invest in U.S. equities have also significantly lagged the U.S. stock indexes. And Canadian bond funds have trailed bond benchmarks in recent years as well.

It's important to note that mutual fund performance numbers don't include the "loads," or sales charges, that some investors pay to buy or sell a mutual fund. If loads were included, the funds' performance numbers would drop significantly.

Why have mutual funds turned in an inferior performance, on average? Largely because of the fees that all mutual funds charge. Canadian equity funds charged an average management expense ratio of 2.19% of assets in 1998. (The management expense ratio, or MER, is the annual percentage of a mutual fund's average assets that the company charges the fund investors for management fees and expenses.) A fund's MER reduces the investment returns of the fund by the amount of the MER. The return you see in the newspapers or on your account statements is what's left after the MER has been subtracted.

For example, an investor with $10,000 in a mutual fund with a 2% MER will be charged about $200 a year. If the stocks in her fund provide a return of, say, 15% one year, the investor will receive a return of only about 13%. As the value of the investment rises, the 2% MER represents an increasing dollar amount.

FUND COMPANIES HAVE OUTPERFORMED THE FUNDS

It's very telling to note that the stocks of the companies that operate the mutual funds have done far better in the 1990s than the mutual funds themselves. A group of mutual fund company stocks returned 39% on average per year for the six years ended Nov. 30, 1996, according to a report by investment firm CIBC Wood Gundy. That's triple the return of the TSE 300 over that period! The stocks are these:

- AGF Management Ltd. (AGF.B-TSE)
- BPI Financial Corp. (BPF-TSE)
- C.I. Fund Management Inc. (CIX-TSE)

- Dundee Bancorp Inc. (DBC.A-TSE) (which operates Dynamic Mutual Funds)

- Investors Group Inc. (IGI-TSE)

- Mackenzie Financial Corp. (MKF-TSE) (operates Industrial, Ivy, Universal, and Star mutual funds)

- Trimark Financial Corp. (TMF-TSE)

Why have these mutual fund company stocks done so well? For the same reason that most mutual funds have underperformed the TSE 300 in recent years—the funds charge high fees! And because Canadians have been pouring their money into mutual funds in the 1990s like never before, the mutual fund companies have been fattening their bottom lines.

This situation is similar to the gambling industry. Whether you play the slot machines, blackjack, baccarat, roulette, or poker, the odds are against you. Smart people stay out of casinos because they know they're bound to lose. Even smarter people stay out of casinos and buy the shares of the companies that operate the casinos. Similarly, smart Canadian investors in the 1990s have stayed away from mutual funds and bought shares of the companies that operate the mutual funds.

WHAT'S THE BIG DEAL ABOUT A 1% SHORTFALL?

But, hey, you might ask, so what if mutual funds are behind the index by a measly 1% or 2% per year? As long as mutual funds provide returns close to the stock indexes they compete with, it doesn't make much difference, right? Wrong!

If a 1% annual shortfall doesn't sound like much to you, consider this example.

$10,000 at 9% = $132,677 over 30 years.
$10,000 at 10% = $174,494 over 30 years.

Over 30 years, a $10,000 investment that returns 9% on average per year would grow to $132,677. The same investment at

10 % would turn into $174,494, almost $42,000 higher! And that's on only $10,000. Think of a 1 % difference over a lifetime of saving and investing. For many Canadians it's likely to amount to hundreds of thousands of dollars!

If you haven't been told about the eye-popping amount of money that you'll need in order to retire comfortably, then take note. It takes many hundreds of thousands of dollars, at least, even to think about retiring these days. A generation from now that will probably rise to millions of dollars! People are living much longer these days, and the government is contributing less and less to your retirement. It's crucial to take financial matters into your own hands.

Let's look at the way a difference of 2 % a year would affect your investment returns.

$10,000 at 8 % = $100,627 over 30 years.
$10,000 at 10 % = $174,494 over 30 years.

An investment of $10,000 that returned 10 % a year would grow to $174,494 in 30 years. An investment of $10,000 that returned 8 % per year would grow to only $100,627! If you're in an underperforming mutual fund for that long, your mutual fund manager will drive past you in his Porsche while you're waiting for the bus!

Here's another example: Say you're a couple in your fifties and you have $500,000 in mutual funds that charge a 2 % management expense ratio (MER). Do you really want to be paying a mutual fund company $10,000 every year just to hold a bunch of stocks and bonds for you? Do you remember how long it took you to save your first $10,000? You could buy 25 of your own stocks for a once-only cost of $625.

BETTERING YOUR ODDS

Investing on your own with a low-fee, long-term strategy tilts the odds of beating most mutual fund returns and capturing that crucial 1 % or more extra annual return in your favour.

There's a perception among many that buying your own stocks is only for that hot tip that Uncle Horace gave you, for the oil exploration company about to hit a gusher, or for the company with the electric comb under development. Not true. You can easily build your own "mutual fund" of big-company shares in Canada and abroad, cost effectively, with no more risk than you take with funds you're already in.

Unfortunately, there are no guarantees that do-it-yourself investing is the ticket to early retirement on your private island in the Caribbean, sipping expensive wines and writing your memoirs by the pool. The only guarantee is that by minimizing the cost of investing, you will have a big advantage: The average diversified, low-fee investment portfolio is likely to outperform the average diversified, high-fee investment portfolio.

THE DISCOUNT-BROKER ALTERNATIVE

Along with the huge growth in mutual fund assets in Canada, another trend is afoot in the financial services industry.

Discount brokers have sprouted up at all the major banks and some other financial institutions, and they're competing like never before. That's caused a sharp drop in the fees they charge, making it economical even for modest-income earners to create their own portfolios. They're also offering more services all the time, such as dividend reinvestment plans (DRIPs) for shares of Canadian companies and increasingly detailed monthly account statements.

Computers and technology are allowing the "little guy" access to the financial markets in a cost-effective manner. You can buy a stock in Canada for $25 or even less at a discount broker, and this figure is likely to drop further. In the United States, for example, some discount brokers offer trading for as low as US$8 a trade. And you don't have to buy a "board lot" of 100 shares. Discount brokers let you buy any number of shares you want for most companies, which allows for investing with small amounts of money.

WHAT THE FUNDS AREN'T TELLING YOU

Because mutual fund profits in Canada are so strong, the industry isn't eager to explain how easy it is for you to learn to invest successfully on your own. You don't hear much about discount brokers from your financial advisor, stockbroker, or mutual fund company. Oh, sure, these people would love to make you a truckload of money from your investments. But their primary motivation is to make money for themselves. It has to be, because if they don't make money they can't stay in business.

How often do the mutual fund companies remind you that most Canadian equity mutual funds have failed to match the performance of the TSE 300 during the 1990s? Not very often. When was the last time you heard a mutual fund promise to give back part of the fees charged to small investors if the fund has a lousy performance? It's very rare, if it happens at all.

And the mutual fund companies rarely remind you how much they're charging you to invest. The average Canadian mutual fund's MER is more than 2% every year, not including any loads charged to buy the fund. There's more than $300 billion invested in Canadian mutual funds today. Every year these funds pocket several billions of dollars in fees, with no recourse if the fund has a bad year, two years, five years, or longer.

Some fee-averse investors have opted for the various no-load mutual funds in Canada. But "no loads" doesn't mean "no fees." It's true that no-load funds don't charge you an upfront, back-end, or declining fee to invest, but all mutual funds charge annual management fees.

Consider this 1998 ad for Altamira mutual funds:

> "We put commissions where other companies don't. In your pocket. Twenty-seven hard-working mutual funds. No loads. And because you never pay commissions, more of what you invest goes into your RRSP. Helping you take control."

This ad doesn't tell the whole story. First, by stating that "you never pay commissions," Altamira may be giving the impression that there's no charge to invest in their funds. But charge you they do. Altamira's flagship equity fund, for example, charged its investors 2.28% in management fees and expenses in 1997, when the fund's return was only 4.1% for the year. That's far below the TSE 300's return of 15% that year. These facts didn't make it into the ad.

Mutual fund companies are very clever at making it appear as if you're not paying a fee to invest. That's because they factor the management fee into the net asset value of the mutual fund every business day. The mutual fund price that you see in the newspaper every day has already had a small amount shaved off to reflect the fees charged. This way, you hardly know you're paying a fee. But over the long term, you're paying handsomely.

The mutual fund companies love to drench the airwaves and newspapers with advertisements. You see businessmen in crisp suits with serious looks on their faces. You see mutual fund managers holding briefcases as they gaze into the horizon looking smart. You see fund managers in meetings with company executives. In the newspapers, you read all about big returns posted by the latest hot fund.

PROMISES, PROMISES

Don't be misled by the sales pitches. These ads rarely mention the sub-par track records of most mutual funds. Poorly performing funds somehow get lost in the shuffle and don't make it into the ads. Fund companies tend to take funds that happen to be performing well and plaster their numbers all over the place, never telling you that the odds of picking a fund that outperforms its benchmark, such as the TSE 300 for Canadian equity funds, are stacked against you.

Further, the ads are full of promises and vague commentary about investing.

- "We expect to consistently outperform the index at lower risk," boasted an ad for new funds from Marathon Performance funds in 1998. (Don't we all!)

- "...we know [our investors will] be happy ten years from now," promised an ad for BPI mutual funds in 1998. (How does BPI know that?)

- "Our complete choice of solutions give you consistently strong performance—now and in the future," said Investors Group in May 1997. (The three biggest of Investors' four Canadian equity funds significantly trailed the TSE 300 index in 1997, 1996, and 1995.)

- "Bottom line: it's what we believe we can make on a Canadian stock," screamed an ad for Templeton mutual funds in 1998. (Bottom line: It's not what you *believe*, it's what the stock actually *does*!)

Many people in the financial services industry want you to think you're incapable of investing on your own—that you need professional help. The Canadian Imperial Bank of Commerce in 1998 urged investors to use their service that buys clients "a portfolio of Canada's best mutual funds selected by experts." This ad came with the added comment: "...guiding you to the right choices, is what truly increases the value of your RRSP investments." The best mutual funds? The right choices? Please throw in tomorrow's winning lotto numbers while you're at it!

Despite what many stockbrokers and fund companies would have you believe, investing on your own doesn't require intimate knowledge of the business and financial world. "The average guy can be a successful investor," says John Bart, a retired professor of finance at the University of Windsor.

YOU CAN DO IT, TOO

You don't need to know the ins and outs of financial statements, goodwill, net present values of future cash flow, or amortization of prepaid contract costs. You won't have to calculate a company's current assets, interest coverage ratio, or debt to total capitalization. Forget about the inventory turnover ratio, depreciation of fixed assets, and minority interest. Leave that arcane stuff to the "pros."

Mutual fund managers know a lot more about finance, accounting, and securities analysis than most people. They know all about moving averages, discounted cash flow, beta, bond duration, bottom-up investing, top-down investing, value investing, growth investing, and momentum investing. Off the tops of their heads, many fund managers can quote you a company's sales figures, profit figures, earnings-per-share figures, cash flow, book value per share, dividend yield, etc. Many mutual fund managers are on a first-name basis with the CEOs of big companies, and they get frequent access to the company's top management. If these fund managers appeared on the game show *Jeopardy*, and every category were Business and Finance, they'd clean up! But guess what? For all their business degrees, hard work, expensive suits, knowledge of companies, big lunch bills, and access to top management, most fund managers aren't able to keep up with the market averages.

You needn't have a deep understanding of a company's operations and products to invest in its stock. Do you understand the finer details of how a digital fibre-optic telephone system works? You probably don't, and neither do most mutual fund managers, but that doesn't stop people from investing in BCE Inc. (BCE-TSE), Bell Canada's parent company, or in Bell's sister company, Northern Telecom Ltd. (NTL-TSE). Do you know enough about mortality rates and probability to head the actuarial department of a life-insurance company? Probably not, but would it stop you or a mutual fund manager from buying shares of Great West Life Assurance Co. (GWO-TSE)? Do you know the ins and outs of designing and building oil and natural-gas pipelines? Thankfully, you don't have to know anything about that before buying shares of Trans-Canada PipeLines Ltd. (TRP-TSE). Are you an expert in getting pie-eyed at the pub every third Tuesday? Maybe you are, but you needn't ever have tasted alcohol to buy shares of Seagram Co. (VO-TSE) or Molson Cos. (MOL.A-TSE)

THE PLAYING FIELD IS LEVEL

Many investors see mutual fund managers as "professionals." With this designation, fund managers and others in the financial services industry are put in the same league as doctors, lawyers, accountants, and highly paid athletes. You probably wouldn't try open-heart surgery on yourself. You wouldn't take out your appendix on the kitchen table. You'd go to a doctor. And you probably wouldn't want to chase the puck into the corner with Eric Lindros on your tail. But when it comes to investing, the facts suggest that anybody has as good a shot as the average mutual fund manager at achieving the returns posted.

What about stockbrokers? Many stockbrokers are genuinely interested in your financial well-being and are doing their best to make you money. Some stockbrokers, however, are slick, aggressive salespeople driven only by earning commissions from their clients. But all stockbrokers must make a substantial amount of money for themselves whether their clients do or not. They have to, or they wouldn't be working for very long. A stockbroker will almost always charge you significantly more to buy a stock than a discount broker will. The reasoning for the higher charge is the research the brokerage house does on the stock they're selling you. This is often the same research the mutual fund managers are reading.

Stockbrokers are happy when you buy and sell often. Every time you buy or sell, they make money. But as we will discuss later, actively switching and selling securities (stocks, bonds, etc.) is the wrong approach.

If you have a stockbroker, take a hard look at the investment returns you have achieved with your broker, including all fees. Was the stockbroker's advice really worth the fees you paid? Could you have picked those stocks yourself with a little education? If so, then why not invest on your own?

How about financial advisors? Financial advisors or financial planners are similar to stockbrokers. Yes, they will give you good advice about financial planning to a certain extent. Usually, however, they will guide you mostly to mutual funds that generate a commission or fee, rather than mutual funds that don't pay them a sales commission. That usually means they'll sell you mutual funds that charge a load or a deferred sales charge. And it often means you wind up in a fund with a high MER, which acts as a drag on your returns.

Let's drop in on a few real people's experiences with financial advisors.

In 1994, Toronto lawyer Jim Lane figured he should get some help managing his money, so he held discussions with several financial advisors to find one he felt comfortable with. "They all struck me as smarmy," Jim says.

He eventually settled with a financial advisor who had done work for Jim's father. The advisor, who was affiliated with a large Canadian brokerage firm, said he would put Jim and his wife's RRSP savings into various mutual funds, and that it wouldn't cost them anything in commissions. That caused Jim to ask the advisor how he made any money selling mutual funds.

"He gave me an answer that I didn't think was very clear," Jim says. Ever since their first meeting, "he hasn't given me any explanation" about how he's compensated for selling mutual funds.

Jim tracked the performance of the dozen or so mutual funds that the advisor sold him. The results to the end of 1997 were "below my expectations," and the savings in the Canadian equity mutual funds he was sold have significantly underperformed Canada's main stock index, Jim noted. As for the financial advisor: "I find it difficult to evaluate whether he knows what he's talking about," Jim says.

Valerie Maday, a Toronto-area teacher, has been with a financial advisor for several years. She invests in mutual funds, but doesn't spend much time with her investments. The concept of investing on her own makes her nervous. "I don't know enough about it, and I don't have enough time," Valerie says. Still, looking at the returns she has received from her mutual funds, she says, "I think I can do better with my money."

As for how mutual funds fees work, Valerie says, "That was explained to me but I didn't retain it." Mutual fund fees are for the fund manager's "expertise," she says. But she was surprised to learn that most mutual funds significantly lag the market averages, and she was shocked to learn about the impact even a 1% difference in annual returns makes on long-term savings.

Valerie's money was invested in two Canadian balanced funds. The funds both had returns below the average Canadian balanced fund for the time she was invested in them. She paid annual fees of 2.24% and 2.37%, no matter what the returns. As if those fees weren't high enough, her financial advisor urged her in early 1998 to buy into another fund that charged a 2.95% annual MER!

HOW DO FINANCIAL ADVISORS MAKE MONEY?

Financial advisors, financial planners, stockbrokers, and the like are usually compensated by the mutual fund companies for the funds they sell. Most advisors are affiliated with a dealer, such as a brokerage firm or a financial planning firm. When an advisor sells a mutual fund with a "front-end load," the load is usually a few percent of the money invested, and this load amount is generally shared by the dealer and the advisor.

Many funds pay trailer fees to advisors who ensure that their clients remain in the mutual fund for a set period of time, such as one year. A typical trailer fee is .25% of the client's assets in the fund. This means your advisor or stockbroker might be collecting a substantial amount of money indirectly from you—even after you've bought the fund!

A popular method of mutual fund sales in Canada is the deferred sales charge (DSC). Many people mistakenly believe that they're not paying to invest if they opt for the deferred sales charge. The DSC means the investor pays no front-end load when buying the fund, but is subject to a sales charge that declines to zero if the investor holds the fund for a set period of time (such as five or seven years). The investor doesn't, however, escape the fund's MER, which is often higher on funds sold by the DSC. Though the investor pays no upfront money with the DSC option, the mutual fund company often pays the dealer as much as 5% of the amount of the investment in the mutual fund at the time of the sale. The dealer shares this money with the advisor.

Such "load" funds sold by brokers and financial advisors account for nearly half of all the money invested in Canadian mutual funds. There are also many "no-load" mutual funds, which are sold by banks and other fund companies and don't charge upfront fees or declining sales charges.

There's no evidence that load mutual funds perform any better than no-loads. In fact, the posted returns of mutual funds that charge a load don't factor in the loads when calculating their returns; if they did, it would significantly reduce those returns.

Loads or no-loads, you're always stuck with the MER that all mutual funds charge. In Canada, the average Canadian equity fund MER was well above 2% in 1998, and the average international fund's MER was about 2.4%.

GOING IT ALONE

You can avoid these high charges by investing on your own. Do-it-yourself investing is easy, fun, educational, and financially rewarding. It takes only a small amount of your time, and you don't have to become a chartered financial analyst to do it right.

There are simple, low-fee ways to invest in the stock markets of Canada, the United States, and several foreign countries without investing in mutual funds. This is through index stocks, which are securities that trade like a stock, but act like a stock index. In a single stock investment, you can own a small piece of all the stocks that make up an index. If you buy a Canadian index stock, you'll own a small piece of all of the big names in Canadian business, such as Royal Bank of Canada (RY-TSE), Canadian Pacific Ltd. (CP-TSE), Hudson's Bay Co. (HBC-TSE), and many others.

Canada has two index stocks. They're called TIPS (R), which stands for Toronto Index Participation Units. TIPS 35 (TIP-TSE) and TIPS 100 (HIP-TSE) are stocks traded on the Toronto Stock Exchange that provide virtually the same returns as the Toronto 35 Index (R) and the TSE 100 (R) Index, respectively. These indexes also have a strong correlation with the performance of the TSE 300, the most widely followed stock-market index in Canada. Buying index stocks takes no more time than investing in mutual funds. Index stocks will be explained in detail in a later chapter.

If, however, you want your Canadian stock investments to have a decent shot at returns above the TSE 300 and the average Canadian equity mutual fund, your investment strategy must go beyond index stocks. This book will show you how to use index stocks as an anchor for a diversified investment portfolio.

In any type of investment strategy, it is crucial to avoid having too much risk. While most mutual funds do indeed offer diversification, it is quite easy to have a diversified portfolio of stocks you've chosen by yourself, even without index stocks. Still, you must avoid recklessly diving into a handful of risky stocks that could destroy your capital.

It's never too soon or too late to invest on your own. Every working Canadian should practise a disciplined saving strategy such as putting aside at least 10% of your after-tax income for savings. Even if you don't make much money, you will probably be surprised how quickly your savings will grow. Soon you will be able to start your own investment portfolio.

For those of you who already have a good-size nest egg, and wonder why some or all of your mutual funds are underperforming, maybe it's time to go it alone. Investing on your own can be done in the same amount of time that many people spend on mutual fund investing, and it incorporates the same concepts, strategies, and tax procedures that mutual fund investors employ.

After all, if you are investing in mutual funds, you must already be taking the time to sort through the ever-growing number of funds. There are more than 1,600 Canadian mutual funds. You can build your own diversified mutual fund by selecting stocks and bonds from a smaller list of candidates.

A WORD TO THE WISE

A few cautionary words before we get started. This is not a get-rich-quick book. This is all about sidestepping the investment fees and taxes that can substantially harm your long-term returns. The premise is that the average diversified, low-fee, long-term-oriented, do-it-yourself investment portfolio is likely to outperform the average mutual fund investment portfolio.

This book is not for GIC types who can't stand any form of losses. Investing in the stock market is risky by nature. However, even GIC worshippers should take note that it's easy to get higher returns by buying Canadian government bonds, which are fully guaranteed by the provinces and the federal government. We'll explore how this is done.

At the time of this writing, North America's and Europe's stocks are trading at some lofty levels indeed, compared with historical norms. U.S. stocks in particular have reached levels deemed by many to be breathtakingly high and ripe for a nasty tumble. Whether owned directly or through mutual funds, stocks have become a high percentage of the average person's total assets in the United States and Canada.

The relentless run-up in stock prices in the 1990s appears to be at least somewhat tied to strong demand for stocks from the baby boomers. Some stock market pundits suggest the boomers' demand for stocks will keep the markets buoyant for another decade, and then they'll ruin the fun by selling out of the stock market when they start to retire from their jobs. Who knows? The party could end a lot sooner than that, or go on even longer. The great bull market (a rising stock market) of the 1990s could come to a crashing halt in an awesome one-day stock-market plunge, or trend lower and lower over a long period of time. The problem with the stock market is that it's a constant giant game of musical chairs, and nobody knows when the music will stop.

That's why every investor should know that the stock market is for long-term investors who don't panic at the first sign of trouble. You should only be invested in the stock market if you can stomach what may be years of flat performance or even significant losses. If you're already into equity mutual funds, then you should already accept this possibility.

For all we know, the world economy is about to collapse and enter a 20-year depression. If it does, then maybe the GIC investors and gold-bar hoarders will be having the last laugh at the rest of us on the breadlines and in the soup kitchens. Somehow, this scenario seems unlikely.

If modern capitalism continues to spread around the world the way it has been for many decades, bringing all the good and bad that goes along with it, then it's the risk-tolerant long-term investors who will reap the rewards.

CHAPTER TWO

Mutual Fund Performance

WHY FUNDS DON'T BEAT THE MARKET

If investing were a marathon race, the mutual fund managers would be carrying bricks while they ran the entire 26 and a quarter miles in a track suit. The higher the fund's management expense ratio, the heavier the brick. Do-it-yourself investors with long-term, diversified approaches would be carrying a hockey puck or two while running the race in shorts and T-shirts. And the market indexes would be prancing along buck naked. (A stock index, also called the market average, is a gauge of a stock market's level based on the prices of the many stocks that make up the index.)

Who will win this race? Statistics and logic indicate that on average the indexes will win, followed by the do-it-yourself investors. Sure, a few of the fittest brick-laden fund managers will place well and make headlines in the newspaper, but most will fall behind the pack. Some will drop out of the race well before finishing.

This is largely because mutual fund investors pay significant fees; do-it-yourself investors pay modest fees, and indexes don't pay any fees. Fees reduce performance.

THE STATISTICS

The statistics are in, and they show that Canadian mutual funds, on average, haven't been able to keep up with the benchmarks they're measured against. The following table shows the average annual compound rates of return for the benchmark TSE 300 total return index, the average Canadian equity mutual fund, and the median Canadian equity mutual fund to Dec. 31, 1997. Both the TSE 300 returns and mutual fund returns assume all dividends or distributions are reinvested. The following mutual fund statistics are based on the mutual fund tables published by *The Globe and Mail*.

	1 Yr	2 Yr	3 Yr	5 Yr	10 Yr
TSE 300 Total Return	15.0%	21.5%	19.1%	17.5%	11.0%
Cdn Equity Fund (Avg)	13.2%	19.1%	16.7%	15.1%	10.2%
Cdn Equity Fund (Median)	13.5%	19.0%	16.5%	14.6%	10.0%

For the 10-year period, only 24 of the 75 equity mutual funds in existence for that period beat the TSE 300 average annual return of 11%. This means that for every fund that topped the TSE 300, more than two fell behind.

For the five-year period, a mere 21 of 123 equity mutual funds beat the TSE 300 average annual return of 17.5%. For every fund that outperformed, nearly five underperformed.

For the three-year period, only 41 of 145 equity mutual funds beat the TSE 300 average annual return of 19.1%.

For the two-year period, only 51 of 156 equity mutual funds beat the TSE 300 average annual return of 21.5%.

And for the one-year period, only 76 of 196 equity mutual funds beat the TSE 300 return of 15%.

And remember that all of the above mutual fund returns exclude any loads paid by the investor! If loads were factored in, the mutual fund returns would be significantly lower.

How do you like your odds of picking a winning mutual fund so far?

Now let's look at yearly performance. The following list shows not only how many Canadian equity mutual funds fell short of the

TSE 300 return in each year shown, but also the average fund return and the median fund return, using data from *The Globe and Mail*.

Year	Funds That Lagged TSE 300	TSE 300 Return	Avg Fund Return	Median Fund Return
1997:	119 of 196 (61%)	15.0%	13.2%	13.5%
1996:	107 of 156 (69%)	28.3%	26.0%	25.2%
1995:	106 of 147 (72%)	14.5%	12.9%	12.5%
1994:	87 of 135 (64%)	0.2%	-2.2%	-2.0%
1993:	76 of 113 (67%)	32.5%	31.6%	29.0%
1992:	38 of 111 (34%)	-1.4%	2.8%	1.3%
1991:	60 of 108 (56%)	12.0%	12.4%	11.6%
1990:	24 of 102 (24%)	-14.8%	-11.3%	-11.8%
1989:	73 of 87 (84%)	21.4%	17.5%	16.9%
1988:	43 of 76 (57%)	11.1%	10.7%	10.4%
1987:	44 of 61 (72%)	5.9%	1.5%	0.6%
1986:	20 of 53 (38%)	9.0%	11.1%	10.8%
1985:	19 of 47 (40%)	25.1%	26.8%	26.4%
1984:	8 of 45 (18%)	-2.4%	1.6%	1.8%
1983:	33 of 41 (80%)	35.5%	31.0%	30.5%

As these returns show, the odds of having picked an outperforming Canadian equity fund, as it turned out, were significantly stacked against you over the past 10 years and longer. These are not good odds when it comes to your hard-earned retirement savings.

You may notice in the table that during 1992, 1990, and 1984, when the TSE 300 fell, more mutual funds outperformed the index than lagged it. This apparent curiosity is likely explained by the fact that, unlike indexes, most mutual funds hold some cash, and cash doesn't fall in value when the stock market does.

Investors should take no comfort in the apparent outperformance of mutual funds over the index in down markets. We invest in stocks because they go up, not down. And any outperformance by mutual funds over the index hasn't caused the funds' long-term performance to keep up with the index. Further, knowing that mutual funds fare better than the index during downturns is only useful if you know the start date and the end date of the next down market. And if you knew that, then you *would* be sipping expensive wines on your island in the Caribbean while writing your memoirs by the pool.

Further, Canadian mutual funds have had the benefit of holding up to 20% of their investments in foreign stocks, while the TSE 300 is entirely made up of good old Canadian stocks. Many Canadian mutual funds pepper their holdings with U.S. stocks, but even the U.S. market's bigger gains haven't kept Canadian mutual funds on par with the TSE.

Despite this benefit, the yearly TSE 300 index still outperformed a significant majority of mutual funds in 10 of the 15 years. Now how do you like your odds?

There was about $83 billion invested in about 230 Canadian equity mutual funds at the end of 1997. The funds charged an average MER (management expense ratio) of about 2.19% every year as of the end of 1997, which represents something on the order of $1.6 billion in fees and expenses getting shaved off those assets by the mutual fund companies in 1997. As the amount of money invested in such mutual funds increases, so will the fees taken by the fund companies. No wonder there are so many mutual funds. It's a lucrative business!

It's important to compare mutual fund returns with total returns of the TSE 300, Canada's most widely followed stock index. All too often, mutual funds compare their performances with each other. This can be misleading, because no matter how the funds perform there will always be a "first quartile" of fund performance. Funds that boast about being in the "first quartile" or "second quartile" aren't measuring themselves with the stock index, which generally outperforms most mutual funds. It's like the guy who's always at the top of the "B" level squash ladder, and refuses to join the "A" level where he belongs.

HOW FEES REDUCE RETURNS

So why did the mutual funds lag the TSE 300 market index by about two percentage points over most of the past 10 years? Could the 2.19% average MER have something to do with it?

"It would be remarkable if [the funds] didn't lag the market by two percentage points," says Malcolm Hamilton, a consulting actuary with William M. Mercer Ltd. in Toronto. (Actuaries spend their days crunching numbers using complex math, statistics, and probabilities to manage risk for pension plans, life-insurance companies, and others.)

"It's clear that if [Canadian investors] didn't pay any fees, then they'd be tracking the market," he says. Mr. Hamilton believes Canadian equity mutual fund fees are too high, and, like a growing number of investors who understand how mutual funds work, he invests on his own.

> With the average Canadian equity fund, "you're paying 2% for less than average performance. The logic of that just escapes me," says John Bart, a retired professor of finance at the University of Windsor and president of the Canadian Shareowners Association. Mutual fund expense ratios have "a material effect" on fund returns, he notes.

The sub-par performance of Canadian mutual funds is no fluke. A major difference between an index and a mutual fund is that a mutual fund charges fees and an index doesn't. Whether or not a mutual fund has an upfront load, a declining load, or a back-end load, you will never escape the annual administration fee that all mutual funds charge. Mutual funds also hold varying amounts of cash, which provides low returns and can harm a fund's results. Funds hold cash in order to pay any investors who sell out, and to pay the expenses of the fund.

If you have an average of $10,000 over the course of a year in a mutual fund with a 2% MER, you'll pay $200 in fees. A $50,000 investment will cost you $1,000 per year; $200,000 will cost $4,000 a year; and so on. These are hefty sums of money that retard the growth of your savings. The mutual fund companies very cleverly factor their MER fees into the price of the mutual fund on a daily basis, which means investors are hardly aware of the money that's streaming out of their accounts. The net asset values of all the mutual funds you see in the daily newspaper have already subtracted that daily fee. Out of sight, out of mind.

> **H**ere's a hypothetical example of how fees charged by mutual funds can eat away at your returns, as calculated by William Mercer's Malcolm Hamilton. If you have RRSP money in a mutual fund with a 2.1% management expense ratio and the investment returns 7% per year for 25 years, the mutual fund's fees and expenses would eat up 39% of the total accumulated amount of money over that time. On a $10,000 investment, say, that would eventually mean $33,066.40 going to the investor and $21,207.90 going to the mutual fund company and its expenses. Yikes.
>
> Even a 1% MER has a significant effect on mutual fund returns. Using the above example with a 1% MER, the investor would wind up with $42,918.70 and the fund company would take $11,355.60 in fees and expenses. A better balance, but still unsavoury for many investors.

Here's another hypothetical example. Let's say Sarah invests $25,000 in the no-load All-Canadian equity fund. Say that 5% of the fund is made up of shares of BCE Inc. (BCE-TSE) on a regular basis. (BCE is one of Canada's biggest companies, and its shares appear in many different Canadian mutual funds. The company owns Bell Canada and part of Northern Telecom Ltd. (NTL-TSE), which is also traded on the stock exchange.) That means Sarah has about $1,250 riding on BCE. The All-Canadian fund charges a 2% MER, so Sarah is paying $500 per year to be invested in the fund, including $25 per year for her stake in BCE alone.

Jill, on the other hand, invests through a discount broker and buys BCE among some other stocks and bonds. BCE is trading at $50, and Jill decides to buy 25 shares, which costs her $1,250 and a one-time commission of $25. Jill's net investment in BCE is $1,225.

Say both Sarah and Jill hang on to their investments for 10 years, during which time BCE provides an average annual return of 10%. Jill enjoys the full extent of the rise of BCE, and after 10 years her investment is worth $3,177.33. Sarah, on the other hand, receives only about 8% per year for her stake in BCE because her mutual fund skims off about 2% of her assets every year. That leaves Sarah with only $2,698.65 invested in BCE in the mutual fund after 10 years, $478.68 less than Jill.

Let's see how a $10,000 investment over 30 years in an average Canadian equity load mutual fund and in a no-load mutual fund would do versus a stock that keeps pace with the TSE 300. Using the actual returns posted by the average Canadian equity fund and the TSE 300 index over the past 10 years as a guide, let's assume the mutual funds return 10% per year, excluding loads, and the stock returns 11% per year.

For a 5% front-end load fund, the actual investment would be $10,000 − $500 = $9,500. With a 3% front-end load, the actual investment would be $10,000 − $300 = $9,700. All of the money in a no-load fund would be invested, as would money invested in a deferred sales charge (DSC) fund that is held for the required amount of time to avoid loads. The stock would require a commission of $25, reducing the net investment to $9,975. For back-end load funds, a few percent would be charged after 30 years, with the effect of front-end loads of the same percentage (as long as the MER was the same).

Here's how much the actual amount invested, including all fees, would become in 30 years if untaxed:

Front-Load Fund Charging 5%:	$165,769
Front-Load Fund Charging 3%:	$169,259
Back-Load Fund Charging 3%:	$169,259
No-Load or DSC Fund:	$174,494
Stock:	$228,351

A load of $500 turned into a shortfall of $8,725 compared with a no-load fund, and a load of $300 turned into a shortfall of $5,235 compared with a no-load fund. But even the no-load fund's return pales in comparison to the stock, which surpassed the no-load fund by $53,857. That's big money!

Some mutual funds that charge a load have lower annual management fees. This is often just a fee trade-off that still winds up costing the investor a lot of money either way. If the fund companies don't get you with the load, they get you with the annual fee.

HOW CASH REDUCES RETURNS

Another thing that can harm mutual fund returns is cash. All mutual funds hold at least a little cash, usually in the form of treasury bills (short-term bonds). Some fund managers are adept at keeping their cash levels low. Others, however, let cash build up in a fund in order to pay fundholders who sell or because the fund manager thinks the stock market will go down. Cash provides low returns. You shouldn't allow significant amounts of your cash to go uninvested. When you invest on your own, it's very important to put any significant amounts of loose cash to work in a stock, a bond, or at least a high-yielding cash account or money-market fund until there's enough to buy another stock or bond.

WHY FUNDS CAN'T KEEP UP

So it's clear that most mutual funds don't keep up with the benchmarks they're supposed to beat. But why not? After all, aren't the people who manage these funds all well educated and highly paid to produce above-average returns?

They are indeed. But it doesn't matter how smart these fund managers are, because mutual funds so dominate the stock market today that they *are* the market. It's therefore impossible for the average mutual fund to outperform the market, since the fund charge fees and the indexes don't.

Everyone is looking for the mutual funds and stocks that will provide the highest returns. But of course, it's impossible for everybody to win the race. There are countless fund managers, financial analysts, advisors, stockbrokers, and investors all playing the same game. They're vying for your investment dollars with sales pitches that make them sound like experts. Which ones should we listen to?

Who the heck knows? The fact is that very few people are able to outperform the market averages consistently. You'll never know today who will be right tomorrow. Only a select few mutual funds have been able to outperform the pack.

The smartest approach, therefore, is to play the game with the lowest possible cost of admission.

WHY FUND FEES ARE SO HIGH

Why do Canadian mutual-fund companies charge so much in fees anyway? Because running a mutual fund is a very complicated operation.

For one thing, you have to hire fund managers. They've got a few degrees and designations under their belts, which means they usually make a lot of money. Then you have to print promotional literature, prospectuses, pamphlets, etc. You have to rent office space and install a complex telephone system and a complex computer system. You have to hire and train staff to answer the phones, respond to investors' questions, and work in the back office. Then you have to hire accountants to keep track of the funds, and pay for legal services. The fund must also be audited every year. Trading costs are substantial, especially for funds that trade actively. Research about companies and stocks is a major cost for many mutual funds. So is advertising. If the fund company's shares are listed on a stock exchange, then listing fees must be paid, and more lawyers and underwriters take a cut. And a major cost for broker-sold or advisor-sold funds is the money paid out to the brokers and advisors.

Then, on top of all this, the fund company has to make a healthy profit to satisfy the investors who own the mutual fund company.

It's all very complicated, but more importantly, it's expensive! Guess who pays? The mutual fund unitholders pay, of course, every day of the week. Why add this unnecessary layer of bureaucracy to your investments?

To be sure, a discount broker has many of the same costs as a mutual fund, and the discount broker wouldn't offer its services unless it could make a good profit. But the added costs of a mutual fund are large. The television, newspaper, and other advertising that many mutual funds pay for can cost millions of dollars per year. And there are only a handful of discount brokers, while there are scores of mutual fund companies. This puts the economy-of-scale factor in favour of discount brokers, because their client bases are larger and growing quickly.

ARE CHANGES COMING?

Don't hold your breath for the Canadian mutual fund industry to drastically cut fees anytime soon. Mutual fund sellers don't want to see their profits drop! A fund is a business product like any other. A business will charge as much as it can get for its product.

Mutual fund MERs, however, will probably edge lower over the years as competition and awareness grow. For example, executives of the large Canadian banks have said that a big reason for their planned mergers is to lower their operating costs and pass those savings on to bank customers. The executives have made a few references to plans to gradually lower mutual fund MERs.

As of spring 1998, the big fund companies hadn't made any such promises to lower their MERs. But they can't ignore the growing awareness among Canadians about mutual fund expenses, or the increased competition for mutual fund sales in the future. This may require a change in the way many mutual funds are sold. Most of the big advisor-sold or broker-sold non-bank mutual funds, which now have billions of dollars of assets, became big because brokers and advisors were eagerly selling those funds and making significant sums in commissions and trailer commissions. These are substantial costs for the fund companies, costs that are often funded by share issues or other such financings. The companies recoup money through MERs, so it's the fund investor who's paying for those significant commissions for brokers and advisors.

Partly because Canadians have been undereducated and complacent about high fund fees, an odd situation has evolved: the equity funds with the most assets and investors are the funds with the highest MERs! And several of these funds have significantly lagged the TSE 300 in recent years.

Clearly, the industry will be forced to change when Canadians demand lower fund costs. The mutual fund companies will have to take action on their costs eventually, and some may well start merging like the banks to help this cause.

But crossing our fingers that mutual funds will reduce their fees to a bare minimum is wishful thinking. And even if the Canadian mutual fund industry scrambles to reduce its annual management fees, they are highly unlikely ever to fall as low as do-it-yourself investing costs.

As we have seen, even a 1 % annual MER can limit long-term growth potential. Do-it-yourself investing with a buy-and-hold approach costs a small fraction of 1 % per year, as does index stock investing. It will likely be several years at least before the average Canadian equity fund's annual management fee drops close to 1 %, if it ever happens. However, there already are a few Canadian equity mutual funds with MERs close to 1 %, which we will discuss later.

Over the past 10 years, many no-load mutual funds sold by the banks and others have gained popularity in Canada. Still, at year-end 1997, about 47 % of Canadian mutual fund money was in funds sold by brokers and dealers. If the U.S. mutual fund industry is any guide, the Canadian mutual fund industry isn't about to make any further dramatic shift to no-load funds. In 1998, many U.S. fund companies actually started to re-emphasize broker-sold load funds. Go figure.

Finally, beware of the growing popularity of fund mergers. Sneaky fund companies will sometimes merge two funds together, and use only the better performing fund's historical performance figures. The poorly performing fund's numbers are dropped from the statistics. This means the average fund performance numbers you see in this book and elsewhere, especially longer-term numbers, are in reality significiantly lower.

C H A P T E R | T H R E E

How the Funds Have Really Done

CANADIAN EQUITY MUTUAL FUND PERFORMANCE

The lagging returns of mutual funds aren't a case of the small funds that nobody buys dragging down the results for the big funds that most Canadians own. Some of the biggest equity funds in Canada have underperformed.

Here are a few of the biggest Canadian equity mutual funds that fell behind the TSE 300 index total return (15%) for 1997.

Were you in any of these funds?

Fund	1997 Returns	Assets
Royal Canadian Equity	12.9%	$3.1 billion
Investors Retirement	10.0%	$3.0 billion
Investors Cdn Equity	9.0%	$3.7 billion
Altamira Equity	4.1%	$2.0 billion
Trimark Select Cdn	3.4%	$5.1 billion
Trimark Cdn	3.2%	$2.3 billion
Trimark RSP Equity	0.6%	$3.2 billion

Each of these funds also lagged the TSE 300's 1996 performance of 28.3%, and only one was able to top the TSE 300's 1995 return of 14.5%.

Of course, one-year returns don't tell the whole story. Let's look at the longer-term performances of the Canadian mutual fund families and larger individual funds for various time periods ended Dec. 31, 1997.

Analysing the results achieved by Canadian mutual funds over the last 10 years is the best way to evaluate the fund industry and the stock market. This is because the industry has changed so dramatically in that time period, growing from less than $50 billion in total assets in 1990 to somewhere around $300 billion at the end of 1997. The number of funds to choose from has soared from about 160 in 1986 to more than 1,200 today. Before the 1990s, only a small percentage of Canadians had money in mutual funds. The number of mutual fund unitholder accounts has jumped from 1.7 million in 1986 to more than 20 million today, according to the Investment Funds Institute of Canada.

Further, the 10-year period that ended in 1997 included many ups and downs in Canada's economy. The economic recession of the early 1990s was one of the worst ever in Canada. Companies across the country underwent wrenching change. The stock market fell sharply in 1990 and was weak in 1992 and 1994, but showed strong gains in 1996, 1993, and 1989. These are the kinds of ups and downs that occur in most 10-year time frames.

Nineteen ninety-seven may go down as the year that several of the country's biggest and best-known mutual funds stumbled badly. All kinds of excuses were made as the 1997 numbers were posted. Fund managers and industry commentators complained that Canadian bank stocks had become too pricey, or that utilities and other dividend-paying stocks were overvalued. Who's to say? These stocks make up a huge portion of the country's overall stock market value and are must-haves for any investor in the Canadian stock market. There's no law that says a bank stock or a utility stock must trade at a certain multiple over the company's earnings. Some mutual fund managers forgot to take their industry's own advice—buy and hold!

Here's a look at some of Canada's big fund families and the funds with established track records.

TRIMARK

Trimark Mutual Funds is one of the grand Pooh-Bahs of Canadian equity mutual funds. During the RRSP season in early 1998, Trimark, as usual, bombarded us with advertisements on television and in newspapers with the hope of getting us to put our savings into their mutual funds. The company is fond of portraying itself as very diligent about studying companies in which it is considering investing. The ads show skeptical fund managers meeting with company executives as the announcer proudly states that Trimark turns down far more investment opportunities than it accepts. "We manage. To Outperform" is Trimark's often-repeated corporate slogan.

An analysis of the facts, however, shows that in 1995, 1996, and 1997, Trimark's Canadian equity funds "Managed. To Underperform. The TSE 300." For all their screening of a company's top management, balance sheet, accounting methods, shop floor, and machinery, Trimark's Canadian equity fund managers weren't able to keep up with the TSE 300 index for three consecutive years.

Three Trimark Canadian equity funds held $10.6 billion of Canadians' money at the end of 1997.

Trimark Canadian Equity Funds — Returns to Dec. 31, 1997:

	1 Yr	2 Yr	3 Yr	5 Yr	10 Yr
Select Canadian Growth	3.4%	12.9%	12.5%	13.9%	
RSP Equity	0.6%	11.4%	10.9%	13.1%	
Canadian	3.2%	14.0%	13.1%	15.3%	12.5%
TSE 300 Returns	15.0%	21.5%	19.1%	17.5%	11.0%

And no front-end loads charged on the Trimark Canadian fund or optional loads on the Select Canadian fund are reflected in these numbers!

At the end of 1997, Trimark Select Canadian Growth had $5.1 billion in assets and charged a 2.3% MER plus an optional load. The Trimark RSP Equity fund had $3.1 billion in assets and charged a 2% MER and a deferred sales charge. And the Trimark Canadian fund had $2.4 billion in assets and charged a 1.5% MER plus a front-end load.

The Trimark fund prospectus contains two full pages outlining "fund expenses," "investor expenses," and "dealer compensation." In 1997, the Select Canadian fund charged a total of $117.1 million in management fees, administration expenses, and tax. The RSP Equity fund charged $71.6 million in management fees and other expenses that year, and the Canadian fund charged $35.3 million in management fees and other expenses. These fees reduce fund performance.

On a yearly basis, Trimark's Select Canadian Growth fund sharply trailed the TSE 300 in 1997, and lagged by several percentage points in 1996 and 1995. The RSP Equity fund also trailed the TSE 300 in 1997, lagged by several percentage points in 1996 and 1995 (but topped the TSE 300 in four of the previous six years). The Trimark Canadian fund sharply trailed the TSE in 1997 and lagged by a few percentage points in 1996 and 1995 (but solidly outperformed the index in most of the fund's previous years).

Trimark's 1997 annual report revealed some interesting points about its Canadian equity funds. First, the funds each held high amounts of short-term investments akin to cash, ranging from 12% to 22% of total assets. Also, the funds had about 5% of their assets in precious metals, an unusual investment for an equity mutual fund. This is an example of an equity mutual fund that has a substantial amount of its money in non-equity investments!

The report also contains a promise in a note co-signed by Trimark's chairman and its chief executive officer: "We have experienced other periods in Trimark's history where short-term results were not good. These did not last, and our superior long-term record remained in place. That will be the case this time as well." This statement came just three paragraphs after another statement in the same note: "No one knows for sure what the markets will do in the future." Hmm.

For many people, three years is not exactly a short-term period. And a mutual fund's promising that future returns will be superior is like a gambler's promising to win the next hand.

INVESTORS GROUP

Let's turn to Investors Group, another woolly mammoth in the Canadian equity mutual fund scene. Four Investors Group Canadian equity funds held $9.5 billion of Canadians' money at the end of 1997.

Investors Group Canadian Equity Funds - Returns to Dec. 31, 1997:

	1 Yr	2 Yr	3 Yr	5 Yr	10 Yr
Canadian Equity	9.0%	16.7%	14.6%	14.7%	11.0%
Retirement Growth	10.8%	16.2%	14.6%	13.8%	
Retirement Mutual Fund	10.0%	16.6%	15.0%	14.4%	9.6%
Investors Summa	23.0%	26.3%	21.8%	16.1%	11.4%
TSE 300 Total Return	15.0%	21.5%	19.1%	17.5%	11.0%

All loads charged by the Equity, Growth, and Mutual funds aren't reflected in these numbers!

None of the first three Investors Group funds was able to top the TSE 300 in a single category over the past 10 years. The Summa fund, however, outpaced the TSE 300 in all but its five-year category. The vast majority of investors' money is in the first three funds, which had assets of $3.8 billion, $2.4 billion, and $3.0 billion, respectively, at the end of 1997. Relatively few investors enjoyed the higher returns of the Summa fund, which had only $290 million in assets at the end of 1997.

Investors' Canadian Equity Fund had a 2.46% MER as reported at the end of 1997, while Retirement Growth's MER was 2.60%, Retirement Mutual's MER was 2.42%, and Summa's MER was 2.46%. Canadian Equity lagged the TSE 300 in six of the 10 years to 1997. Retirement Growth lagged the TSE 300 in four of its eight years of existence, and Retirement Mutual lagged the TSE 300 in seven of the 10 years to 1997. Summa lagged the TSE 300 in five of its 10 years of operating.

Investors Group operates by selling its mutual funds through its own force of salespeople, or investment advisors, who are known for their personal approach and relationship building. They often travel to people's homes to sell them Investors Group mutual funds and talk about investing. Unfortunately, such relationships don't improve investment returns.

MACKENZIE FINANCIAL/INDUSTRIAL FUNDS

On to mutual fund giant Mackenzie Financial Corp., which runs the Industrial, Ivy, and Universal funds, among others. The following funds held about $7.3 billion of Canadians' money at the end of 1997:

	1 Yr	2 Yr	3 Yr	5 Yr	10 Yr
Industrial Future	14.4%	15.3%	16.3%	20.0%	10.2%
Industrial Growth	-1.5%	8.9%	7.9%	12.7%	7.1%
Industrial Horizon	14.7%	17.6%	13.9%	16.0%	9.2%
Ivy Canadian Fund	17.6%	21.3%	19.5%	14.7%	
Mackenzie Sentinel Cda	0.9%	13.0%	7.8%	15.9%	8.0%
TSE 300 Total Return	15.0%	21.5%	19.1%	17.5%	11.0%

Loads aren't included in these numbers!

The Industrial funds fell short of the TSE 300 for every category except the Future fund's 20.0% five-year return, which was a solid performance. The Ivy fund, the biggest of the Mackenzie Canadian equity funds, has been strong in recent years, but its five-year number trails the TSE 300. The 1997 MERs for the five funds in the above chart are, in order: 2.38%, 2.37%, 2.37%, 2.38%, and 1.99%. The Sentinel fund is small, with only $11 million in assets.

Looking at yearly returns, the Future fund lagged the TSE 300 in seven of its 10 full years of operating, and the Growth fund lagged the TSE 300 in eight of its past 10 years. Horizon lagged the TSE 300 in six of its 10 full years of operating. The Ivy Canadian fund topped the TSE in three of its five full years of operating.

ALTAMIRA

Altamira shook up the Canadian mutual fund industry in the early 1990s by posting some hot returns and drawing a ton of money into its no-load mutual funds.

	1 Yr	2 Yr	3 Yr	5 Yr	10 Yr
Equity	4.1%	10.4%	11.8%	15.8%	19.7%
Capital Growth	7.8%	9.1%	9.1%	11.9%	11.5%
AltaFund Investment	-12.6%	12.5%	12.1%	14.1%	
North American Recovery	25.9%	27.7%	18.3%		
TSE 300 Total Return	15.0%	21.5%	19.1%	17.5%	11.0%

The $2.0 billion Altamira Equity Fund significantly lagged the TSE 300 in 1997 and 1996, but a long stretch of outperformance in previous years has kept the 10-year number exceptionally strong. The much smaller Capital Growth fund has fallen sharply behind the TSE 300 in recent years, but some solid years in the early 1990s have kept its 10-year number strong. The $210 million AltaFund has been very volatile, smartly topping the TSE 300 in three of its six full years of operation. Still, a nasty tumble in 1997 dragged its five-year number well below the TSE 300. The $133 million Recovery fund has topped the TSE 300 in recent years, but a bad 1995 performance kept its three-year return below the TSE 300.

In early 1998 Altamira reminded us in its advertisements that the Equity Fund has substantially outperformed the TSE over 10 years. "Two words that describe the investment philosophy of the Altamira Equity Fund. Long Term."

The ads don't note, however, that the Equity Fund had only $569.8 million in assets at the start of 1993, a year in which the fund increased its assets by nearly $1 billion. Investors in the fund from the start of 1993 to the end of 1997 have significantly lagged the TSE 300. This raises a question: just how many investors benefitted from the strong 10-year Equity Fund performance that Altamira continues to advertise, compared with the number of investors whose returns have lagged the index in recent years?

Finally, for Altamira to describe its Equity Fund's investment philosophy as "long term" is strange because the fund is famous for actively trading its stocks and frequently rotating its investments from one industry to another. Altamira changed the management of its Equity Fund in May 1998.

AGF

Another family of Canadian equity mutual funds is run by AGF:

	1 Yr	2 Yr	3 Yr	5 Yr	10 Yr
Canadian Equity	0.5%	10.6%	11.1%	10.4%	6.1%
Canadian Growth	15.6%	15.9%	13.6%	13.6%	
Growth Equity	17.1%	23.1%	20.1%	19.9%	12.9%
TSE 300 Total Return	15.0%	21.5%	19.1%	17.5%	11.0%

The numbers don't reflect any loads charged!

The Canadian Equity fund had $721 million in assets at the end of 1997, while Canadian Growth had $350 million and Growth Equity had $888 million. The Canadian Equity fund substantially underperformed the TSE for each category, and the Canadian Growth fund lagged the TSE for all but the one-year category. The Growth Equity fund has outperformed the TSE in each category. The funds' MERs in 1997 were, in order, 2.95%, 2.43%, and 2.80%.

Looking at yearly results, AGF Canadian Equity lagged the TSE 300 in nine of the 10 years to 1997, while AGF Canadian Growth lagged in four of its eight full years of operating. The Growth Equity fund topped the TSE 300 in five of 10 years, and has been very profitable for investors who could handle the fund's high volatility.

C.I.

The C.I. family of funds has two main Canadian equity funds:

	1 Yr	2 Yr	3 Yr	5 Yr	10 Yr
Canadian Growth	6.0%	10.7%	11.0%		
Canadian Sector Shares	5.2%	9.9%	10.2%	15.3%	7.0%
TSE 300 Total Return	15.0%	21.5%	19.1%	17.5%	11.0%

Any loads paid would make these numbers lower!

The Canadian Growth fund, with $961 million in assets, is far bigger than the $45 million Sector fund, even though Sector is much older. Canadian Growth substantially lagged the TSE 300 index in 1997, 1996, and 1995, and was slightly ahead of the TSE 300 in 1994. Sector Shares lagged the TSE 300 index in seven of its 10 full years of operating. The MERs of the two funds were 2.38% and 2.43% respectively in 1997.

DYNAMIC

The Dynamic group of mutual funds has two main Canadian equity funds:

	1 Yr	2 Yr	3 Yr	5 Yr	10 Yr
Dynamic Canadian Growth	0.8%	14.3%	10.9%	20.1%	13.7%
Dynamic Fund of Canada	10.9%	15.9%	12.2%	13.9%	10.6%
TSE 300 Total Return	15.0%	21.5%	19.1%	17.5%	11.0%

No loads are factored into these numbers!

The Dynamic Canadian Growth fund had $816 million in assets and a 2.49% MER in 1997, while the Dynamic Fund of Canada had $253 million in assets and an MER of 2.47%. Canadian Growth has topped the TSE 300 index in five of its past 10 years, and stellar returns in 1993, 1992, and 1991 have held up its long-term numbers despite lagging returns in 1997 and 1995. Dynamic Fund of Canada lagged the TSE 300 index in six of its 10 years through 1997.

GREEN LINE

Green Line is the discount broker and mutual fund arm of Toronto Dominion Bank. Three no-load Green Line funds are devoted to the Canadian stock market, as is an index fund that we'll look at in a moment.

	1 Yr	2 Yr	3 Yr	5 Yr	10 Yr
Blue Chip Equity	15.1%	20.6%	17.8%	12.9%	8.9%
Canadian Equity	24.4%	25.0%	19.6%	18.0%	
Value	17.2%	31.8%	24.6%		
TSE 300 Total Return	15.0%	21.5%	19.1%	17.5%	11.0%

These funds had more than $2 billion invested at the end of 1997, and had MERs of 2.27%, 2.11%, and 2.13%, respectively. The Blue Chip fund lagged the TSE 300 index in seven of its 10 years of operations, while Canadian Equity lagged in five of nine years. The Value fund topped the TSE 300 index in two of its four full years of operating.

PHILLIPS HAGER & NORTH

One of the bigger groups of non-bank no-load funds is offered by Phillips Hager & North (PH & N).

	1 Yr	2 Yr	3 Yr	5 Yr	10 Yr
Canadian Equity	14.2%	21.9%	18.9%	17.4%	11.8%
Canadan Equity Plus	12.9%	20.5%	17.9%	16.7%	12.0%
Vintage	17.3%	27.8%	25.2%	20.4%	17.0%
TSE 300 Total Return	15.0%	21.5%	19.1%	17.5%	11.0%

The PH&N funds have had solid returns, and all three 10-year returns were ahead of the TSE. At the end of 1997, the Canadian Equity fund, with $706 million in assets, had more than twice as much money as the other two funds combined, and has roughly tracked the TSE 300's performance.

Canadian Equity topped the TSE 300 in six of 10 years through 1997, as did the Equity Plus fund. Vintage outperformed the TSE 300 in a remarkable eight of the 10 years through 1997.

Solid returns aren't all that sets PH&N apart. The company has some of the lowest annual management fees in the Canadian mutual fund industry. In 1997, the Canadian Equity fund's MER was 1.09%, Equity Plus charged 1.18%, and Vintage charged 1.76%. The strong returns aren't sheer coincidence. A low MER means a fund manager has a much better shot at meeting or exceeding the market averages, compared with managers whose funds have higher MERs. Still, your fees can be even lower than PH&N's if you invest on your own!

SPECTRUM UNITED

	1 Yr	2 Yr	3 Yr	5 Yr	10 Yr
Canadian Equity*	13.8%	n/a	15.7%	17.0%	12.7%
Canadian Investment	24.0%	25.6%	22.3%	16.1%	9.6%
Canadian Stock	18.4%	20.3%	17.1%	14.5%	8.5%
TSE 300 Total Return	15.0%	21.5%	19.1%	17.5%	11.0%

Spectrum's loads aren't included in these numbers.

The Spectrum United Canadian Equity fund had $1.3 billion in assets at the end of 1997, compared with less than $200 million for each of the other two funds. The Canadian Equity fund lagged the TSE 300 in recent years, but still maintained strong longer-term returns. The Investment fund, on the contrary, has had good recent returns but fell behind the TSE 300 for the five-year and 10-year periods. The Stock fund has mostly lagged the TSE 300.
* Performance numbers as posted in Spectrum United advertisement. Returns prior to Nov. 1, 1996 relate to United Canadian Equity Fund.

AIC

Probably the hottest Canadian mutual fund in the 1990s has been the AIC Advantage fund. AIC's strong performance in recent years has caused an explosion in the company's assets under management, as more and more Canadians seek a piece of the big returns.

	1 Yr	2 Yr	3 Yr	5 Yr	10 Yr
AIC Advantage	43.3%	54.4%	46.1%	35.1%	21.9%
AIC Diversified Canada	32.1%	47.7%	40.1%		
TSE 300 Total Return	15.0%	21.5%	19.1%	17.5%	11.0%

These numbers don't include any loads paid.

The Advantage Fund's returns are what Canadian mutual fund investors drool for. The fund flew past the TSE 300 in six of the 10 years through 1997, while Diversified beat the TSE 300 in each of its three full years of operating. The funds had MERs of 2.56% and 2.69% respectively, and assets of $1.8 billion and $1.1 billion in 1997. (A newer fund, AIC Advantage II, had an astounding $3.3 billion in assets at the end of 1997.)

How has AIC done it? Two words: mutual funds. Very cleverly, the AIC Advantage fund invested heavily in financial services companies, including Trimark and several of the other companies that operate the Canadian mutual funds we're discussing in this book! So here we have the situation where a mutual fund is making a killing by buying shares of other mutual fund companies. Very smart, but how long will it last?

INDEX FUNDS

What about index funds? Index funds aren't like "actively managed" equity funds, because index funds in Canada simply mimic the TSE 300; they buy the exact same stocks that are in the index and in the same proportion. But guess what? Not even index funds have actually kept up with the index, because they all charge significant annual fees and hold some cash.

Index Fund	1 Yr	2 Yr	3 Yr	5 Yr	10 Yr
CIBC Cdn Index	14.0%				
First Cdn Index	13.5%	19.8%	17.3%	15.3%	
Green Line Index	13.7%	20.0%	17.7%	16.1%	9.5%
GWL Equity Index DSC	12.3%	18.6%	16.2%		
GWL Equity Index NL	12.0%	18.2%	15.9%	14.5%	
NN Canadian 35 Index	13.2%	19.5%	16.5%	14.7%	

Index Performances					
TSE 300 Total Return	15.0%	21.5%	19.1%	17.5%	11.0%
TSE 100 Total Return	15.0%	21.6%	19.2%	17.4%	11.1%
Toronto 35 Total Return	16.4%	23.0%	20.2%	17.9%	11.3%

No surprises here. The index funds fell significantly behind the indexes. These funds charge annual MERs ranging between 1% and 2.6%. You can avoid these fees by buying one or both of the TIPS index stocks, which track the Toronto 35 and the TSE 100 indexes much more closely than any index mutual fund. The Toronto 35 and TSE 100 indexes are highly correlated with the returns of the TSE 300. (We will discuss TIPS in detail in "Index Stocks: Mutual Funds without the fees.")

OTHER CANADIAN EQUITY FUNDS

Now let's quickly look at some of the other bigger Canadian equity funds with at least five-year track records. Their long-term results were, for the most part, behind the TSE 300 for the periods ending in 1997. Some funds are no-load, while others charge a load.

	1 Yr	2 Yr	3 Yr	5 Yr	10 Yr
Atlas Cdn Large Cap	26.7%	28.2%	22.7%	16.6%	10.4%
BPI Cdn Equity Value	14.9%	19.9%	18.0%	13.0%	
CIBC Cdn Equity	16.5%	18.5%	14.8%	12.0%	
Cda Life Cdn Equity	10.6%	17.9%	16.5%	13.7%	9.9%
Cda Trust Stock	18.4%	20.4%	16.5%	14.3%	
Co-operators Cdn Eqty	18.7%	20.6%	16.7%	15.3%	
Dejardins Action	15.1%	18.1%	16.0%	14.0%	9.1%
Elliot Page Equity	-1.9%	10.5%	14.4%	14.1%	
Fidelity Capital Builder	3.0%	10.2%	11.8%	10.4%	
Global Strategy Growth	15.0%	19.2%	16.0%	13.9%	
Guardian Growth	9.6%	23.8%	18.2%	16.4%	
Great West Cdn Equity	13.2%	18.0%	15.5%	13.7%	
ICM Equity	6.5%	13.0%	12.9%	14.5%	9.9%
InvesNat Cdn Equity	1.8%	13.1%	14.0%	12.8%	
London Life Cdn Equity	17.2%	23.7%	19.3%	16.1%	10.8%
Maritime Life Growth AC	15.8%	22.0%	19.1%	15.6%	9.3%
Maxxum Cdn Equity Growth	0.0%	11.3%	16.0%	16.0%	10.7%
MD Equity	16.7%	19.1%	14.9%	16.5%	10.7%
Mutual Equifund	10.7%	18.3%	18.0%	14.5%	9.0%

	1 Yr	2 Yr	3 Yr	5 Yr	10 Yr
Mutual Premier BlueChip	10.1%	17.9%	16.5%	13.0%	
National Trust Cdn Eqty	17.5%	21.0%	16.2%	13.5%	9.9%
Royal Canadian Equity	12.9%	17.3%	15.9%	15.4%	9.0%
Royal Life Equity	21.3%	23.1%	19.5%	15.8%	
Scotia Excelsior CdnBlue	6.3%	14.5%	12.3%	10.0%	8.4%
Scotia Excelsior CdnGrow	6.8%	19.9%	19.8%	17.5%	11.0%
Strategic Value CdnEqty	14.0%	16.4%	14.3%	12.2%	8.0%
Talvest Canadian Equity	13.0%	15.1%	14.1%	12.4%	9.5%
Templeton Cdn Stock	17.5%	20.6%	16.0%	16.4%	
TSE 300 Total Return	15.0%	21.5%	19.1%	17.5%	11.0%

THE OUTPERFORMERS

We've looked at the large fund families and seen that most funds have lagged the market averages, while a few have performed well. But weren't there other funds that outperformed the index? Yes there were. Here are some of the bigger Canadian equity funds that have consistently outperformed the TSE 300 or maintained above-average long-term returns through 1997.

	1 Yr	2 Yr	3 Yr	5 Yr	10 Yr
ABC Fundamental Value	20.3%	25.9%	20.8%	32.1%	
Bissett Canadian Equity	31.5%	33.7%	27.7%	22.1%	15.3%
Clean Environment Eqty	34.3%	32.9%	29.0%	21.1%	
Ethical Growth	17.4%	22.7%	20.9%	17.2%	12.2%
GBC Canadian Growth	27.0%	31.1%	25.9%	20.1%	
McLean Budden Pooled	18.6%	29.8%	24.8%	19.7%	14.2%
National Equities	19.9%	24.8%	20.5%	17.9%	11.1%
Standard Life Ideal	19.5%	23.2%	21.5%	17.3%	11.3%
Tradex Equity	19.0%	27.3%	23.8%	19.5%	12.1%
TSE 300 Total Return	15.0%	21.5%	19.1%	17.5%	11.0%

The ABC fund outperformed the TSE 300 in seven of its eight full years through 1997. Bissett topped the TSE 300 in eight of 10 years through 1997. GBC outpaced the TSE 300 in eight of its nine full years through 1997. McLean Budden beat the TSE 300 in eight of 10 years through 1997.

Is it a fluke that these managers topped the TSE 300 so often? It's hard to say. It appears that amid all the chaos in the financial markets, there are some money managers who can regularly outpace the pack. Unfortunately, however, consistently above-average mutual fund managers are a rare breed, and there's no guarantee that their hot streaks will continue. We've already looked at some once-hot funds that have stumbled badly in recent years. Sometimes hot performance numbers cause a surge of new money into a fund, which can throw a fund manager's winning strategy off course or cause the fund's cash level to rise.

Also, several of the above funds have minimum investment restrictions. ABC, for example, requires at least a $150,000 investment. Others are more like $5,000 or $10,000.

There are some lessons to learn from the funds that have outperformed the TSE 300. The first is that the outperformers tend to have lower annual fees. For example, the Phillips Hager & North Canadian equity funds had MERs ranging from 1.09% to 1.76% in 1997, well below the average MER of 2.19%. The Bissett Canadian Equity fund's MER in 1997 was 1.33%. McLean Budden Pooled Canadian had an MER of 1.0%, and the Tradex Equity MER was 1.35%. Another fund not mentioned so far is the Scudder Canadian Equity fund, which had an average annual compound return of 40.2% for one year and 36.8% for the two years ended Dec. 31, 1997. The fund had a 1997 MER of 1.25%.

As low as these fees are, you can make yours even lower by investing on your own!

OTHER TYPES OF FUNDS

Moving beyond Canadian equity funds, let's now look at Canadian dividend funds, small-cap funds, precious metal funds, and resource funds.

DIVIDEND FUNDS

There were about 50 dividend funds in operation at the end of 1997. They invest primarily in common stocks that pay solid dividends and preferred shares. Partly because interest rates have fallen sharply over the past few years, stocks that pay good dividend rates have increased in value.

Here are the average annual compound rates of return for dividend funds to the end of 1997, according to *The Globe and Mail*'s mutual fund survey, compared with the TSE 300 total returns:

	1 Yr	2 Yr	3 Yr	5 Yr	10 Yr
Dividend Funds	20.8%	23.3%	20.2%	15.2%	11.1%
TSE 300	15.0%	21.5%	19.1%	17.5%	11.0%

Clearly, the place to be in the past few years was in funds that invested in dividend-paying stocks. An even better place to be, however, was in the dividend-paying stocks themselves, since you would have sidestepped the funds' 1.85% average MER. At the end of 1997 there was about $16 billion invested in about 50 dividend funds.

Buying stocks that pay a dividend is easy to do. It's as simple as looking in the newspaper for companies with good dividend yields. The dividend yield is the company's annual dividend per share divided by the current price of the stock. The Appendix in this book will also show you which stocks have traditionally paid good dividends.

Canada's dividend funds hold many of the same stocks that appear in regular equity mutual funds. Take, for example, the Bank of Montreal's First Canadian Dividend Income Fund, which had 86% of its $99 million in assets invested in only 27 stocks on Sept. 30, 1996. These names include Moore Corp. (MCL-TSE), the big business forms maker; pipeline operators Enbridge Inc. (ENB-TSE); TransCanada PipeLines Ltd. (TRP-TSE); and Westcoast Energy Inc.

(WE-TSE). It includes the following utilities: BC Gas Inc. (BCG-TSE), BC Telecom Inc. (BCT-TSE), BCE Inc. (BCE-TSE), Canadian Utilities Inc. (CU.A-TSE), Nova Scotia Power Inc. (NSP-TSE), phone company Telus Corp. (AGT-TSE), and power producer Transalta Corp. (TA-TSE). It also includes Thomson Corp. (TOC-TSE), one of the world's biggest information providers; and five of Canada's banks.

Most of these stocks have risen greatly in value in recent years, which has caused their dividend yields to fall. Partly for this reason, it is very unlikely that these stocks will continue in the near term to deliver the hot returns they have been posting. A dividend yield of 5% or 6% was considered standard for a typical dividend-paying common stock just a few years ago. Today you're doing well if you get 3% on your dividend-paying common stocks, and 6% for a preferred share.

MERs of dividend funds haven't been an issue with most investors recently. Who cares if the past year's return was 24% instead of 26%? But MERs will be more important for investors in the years to come. With the prospect of dividend-paying stocks cooling down considerably and sporting lower dividend yields over the next several years, a 1.85% MER could prove to be a serious drag on returns. In fact, it will eat up a big chunk of the dividends being paid by these stocks!

To be sure, there are some no-load dividend funds with relatively low MERs:

Fund	MER
Royal Monthly Income	1.12%
Saxon High Income	1.25%
Scotia Excelsior Dividend	1.07%
MD Dividend	1.29%
Bisset Dividend Income	1.50%

Still, instead of paying these fees every year you could pay them just once by buying your own dividend-paying stocks and pocketing all the dividends and capital gains for yourself!

SMALL-CAP AND MID-CAP FUNDS

Another group of Canadian equity funds is small-cap and mid-cap mutual funds.

> The "cap" in small-cap is short for capitalization. A company's market capitalization is its latest stock price multiplied by the number of shares the company has outstanding. It's also the value that the stock market is putting on the company. These days a small market capitalization is considered to be a few hundred million dollars or less. Companies valued at about $500 million or so are in the mid-cap range.

Small-cap stocks, as the name implies, are shares of relatively small companies. They usually aren't included in the TSE 300. These companies are often developing a new product or drug for the medical industry, a new software program, or a new high-tech gadget. Countless small companies also operate in the various natural resources industries, such as drilling for oil and natural gas, or mining gold or other metals. But a small-cap company could be in any line of business.

Some stock-market pundits believe small caps are the place to be because small companies can grow faster than big ones. The small caps, they say, have higher risk but offer bigger returns. This is debatable, but has proven to be true during some periods over the years. There was about $12 billion invested in 72 small-cap funds at the end of 1997. Here's the average annual compound returns for small-cap funds to the end of 1997, according to *The Globe and Mail* survey:

Small-Mid-Cap Funds	1 Yr	2 Yr	3 Yr	5 Yr	10 Yr
Median Return	15.0%	21.8%	19.2%	14.6%	12.1%
Average Return	11.6%	20.6%	19.1%	16.7%	10.8%
TSE 300 Return	15.0%	21.5%	19.1%	17.5%	11.0%

As you can see, the average small-cap fund's return has been quite similar to the TSE 300. The range of returns, however, is quite different. Some of the best small-cap funds posted average annual returns above 30% for a few years in a row. The worst, however, produced substantial negative returns. These funds often make one-year moves in the 50%, 75%, 100% range or more, and suffer breathtaking drops as well. Clearly, these funds aren't for the faint of heart.

Small-cap mutual funds tend to charge even higher fees than regular equity mutual funds, ostensibly for the extra work that goes into choosing good investments from a sea of small-cap choices. The above funds had an average MER of 2.37%.

Well-known fund companies were among the best and the worst performers in the small-cap arena. The biggest small-cap/mid-cap fund is run by Fidelity; its Canadian Growth Company fund held $1.2 billion at the end of 1997. The fund's three-year average annual compound rate of return to the end of 1997 was a solid 26.7%.

The no-load Bissett Small Cap fund returned an enviable 33.8% on average per year for the five years through 1997, while Multiple Opportunities returned 35.6% per year over the same period. The Marathon Equity fund returned 30.4% per year for the five years through 1997, and 22.0% per year for the 10 years through 1997. Other notable five-year returns were posted by Guardian Enterprise A (20.1%), Mawer New Canada (23.0%), Sceptre Equity Growth (26.6%), and Spectrum United Canadian Growth (22.3%).

SMALL CAP, BIG RISK?

It's for these types of returns that many investors are attracted to small-cap mutual funds. Unfortunately, risk increases with small companies, and not all funds are runaway winners. Several funds posted significant losses in 1997, including BPI Canadian Small Companies, Industrial Equity Fund Ltd., Multiple Opportunities, Cambridge Growth, and Cambridge Special Equity, though the longer-term returns for some of these funds were solidly positive.

S o despite this book's title, it is probably a good idea to include a small-cap Canadian equity fund or two as a small part of your equity investment portfolio, say 10% to 25%. This strategy increases diversification and offers potentially higher returns. Whereas it's easy to build your own portfolio of "big-cap" Canadian and international equities with index stocks and/or individual stocks, it's much more difficult for the individual investor to run around looking for small-cap stocks.

When shopping for a small-cap fund, look for no-load funds with low MERs and decent track records. Few, if any, widely available no-load Canadian small-cap mutual funds had exceptionally low MERs as of year-end 1997, but some (such as Altamira Special Growth, Bissett Small Cap, Mawer New Canada, and Saxon Small Cap Fund) had MERs below 2.0%. Some funds have minimum-investment restrictions.

PRECIOUS METALS AND NATURAL RESOURCE FUNDS

At the end of 1997, more than 40 Canadian mutual funds were devoted to investments in gold mining and natural resource companies, such as oil and gas or forestry concerns. Their track records over the past 10 years are abysmal, as shown by *The Globe and Mail's* survey of these funds.

	1 Yr	2 Yr	3 Yr	5 Yr	10 Yr
Median Return	-25.6%	-4.1%	1.6%	10.7%	3.0%
Average Return	-24.8%	-0.6%	2.4%	10.2%	3.2%
TSE 300 Return	15.0%	21.5%	19.1%	17.5%	11.0%

Not surprisingly, there's no great rush to get into these funds, which held about $3 billion at the end of 1997. A host of unfavourable factors combined to make resource stocks the dogs of the Canadian investment scene over the past 10 years and longer. A big factor is that prices for the gold, nickel, copper, oil, aluminum, lumber, pulp, paper, and similar commodities that these companies sell haven't appreciated in many years. Many resource-company stocks tend to go up and down like a see-saw, never going anywhere. That's why they're called "cyclical."

To be sure, resource stocks do have their day in the sun, but it never seems to last very long. Resource-based mutual funds shot up an average of 73% in 1993. Those returns, however, were sandwiched between several years of losses or meagre gains. We'll discuss resource or cyclical stocks in depth later.

U.S. EQUITY FUNDS

Turning now to the international stock-market scene, let's first look at funds that invest in the land of the free, and home of the brave, the United States. The U.S. stock market is second to no other country's in terms of size, diversity, liquidity, and, most important, performance. Here's how Canadian mutual funds that invest there have performed against the country's main benchmark, the S&P 500 index, to Dec. 31, 1997, as surveyed by *The Globe and Mail*:

	1 Yr	2 Yr	3 Yr	5 Yr	10 Yr
Funds' Median Return	29.3%	23.5%	24.4%	17.0%	13.7%
Funds' Average Return	27.7%	22.1%	23.0%	16.3%	13.5%
S&P 500 Return*	39.2%	31.1%	32.0%	23.1%	19.1%

(*Return calculated in Canadian dollars by Datastream.)

There were about 144 funds with at least a one-year track record that invested primarily in the United States. Only 14 of them were able to top the 39.2% performance put on by the S&P 500. In the five-year category, all but two of 54 funds were able to outperform the S&P 500. The average MER for these funds in 1997 was 2.22%.

As impressive as the average fund's return is over the various time periods, it is well behind the index in every category. The same story is true of U.S.-based mutual funds that invest in the U.S. stock market. To the end of 1997, the S&P hadn't had a down year since 1990, an incredible feat. It appears that the longer and higher the stock market climbs, the further behind most mutual funds fall.

Now which would you rather do—buy an actively managed mutual fund with the odds stacked against you, or buy a single stock that is virtually guaranteed to keep up with the index? Just like Canada's TIPS stocks, the U.S. has index stocks that track the S&P 500 and the Dow Jones Industrial Average. We will discuss these in "Index Stocks: Mutual Funds Without the Fees."

INTERNATIONAL EQUITY FUNDS

International Equity Funds invest in stocks around the globe, and most are not eligible for RRSPs except for foreign content. Here's how they've done according to *The Globe and Mail* survey.

	1 Yr	2 Yr	3 Yr	5 Yr	10 Yr
Median Return	12.6%	12.8%	12.2%	13.7%	10.5%
Average Return	12.0%	12.8%	11.4%	13.0%	10.1%
MSCI World*	21.3%	17.9%	17.9%	18.7%	12.2%
TSE 300 Return	15.0%	21.5%	19.1%	17.5%	11.0%

(*Morgan Stanley Capital International World index calculated in Canadian dollars by Datastream.)

Many investment advisors emphasize the need to invest globally for broad diversification. This is good advice. Canadians had more than $43 billion invested in about 156 international equity mutual funds in 1997. These funds had an average MER of 2.41% in 1997, representing an annual take of something in the neighbourhood of $1 billion for the mutual fund companies, not including loads.

Let's take a look at the international equity funds that had more than $750 million in assets at the end of 1997. Remember that any loads paid by investors in these funds would make the returns significantly lower.

	1 Yr	2 Yr	3 Yr	5 Yr	10 Yr
AGF Int'l Value	23.6%	21.3%	19.2%		
C.I. Global	21.1%	18.3%	13.3%	14.1%	11.3%
Fidelity Int'l Portfol	24.1%	20.0%	18.1%	18.8%	13.1%
Investors Global	16.6%	15.1%	14.6%	14.3%	9.8%
Investors North Amer	13.9%	16.6%	16.6%	14.4%	14.0%
Investors World Growth	-0.4%	5.0%	6.2%		
MD Growth	21.1%	20.8%	18.9%	19.2%	13.7%
Templeton Growth	17.1%	17.7%	16.5%	17.5%	14.7%
Templeton Int'l Stock	15.9%	18.7%	16.5%	19.8%	
Trimark Fund	16.0%	15.4%	15.8%	18.6%	17.4%
Trimark Select Growth	12.6%	13.3%	13.6%	16.2%	
MSCI index	21.3%	17.9%	17.9%	18.7%	12.2%

The bigger international equity funds fared much better than the average international fund, an encouraging situation for the average investor. Some funds even outperformed the MSCI index. Many funds achieved this by avoiding Japan's stock market, which hadn't appreciated by the end of 1997 since collapsing in the early 1990s. The MSCI index includes a hefty component of Japanese stocks, since Japan's stock market remains the world's second biggest after the U.S.

Canadians are attracted to international funds because they offer broad diversification and historically higher returns. In the last few years the American Stock Exchange has developed index stocks for 17 countries and plans to launch 11 more. These index stocks make international investing a snap at a cost far less than the average international equity fund. More on this later.

BOND FUNDS

Now on to fixed-income investments. Besides stock mutual funds, there is a plethora of bond funds and other fixed-income mutual funds available to Canadians. Here's how the median and average bond fund performed compared with some bond-market benchmarks, according to *The Globe and Mail* survey.

CANADIAN BOND FUNDS

	1 Yr	2 Yr	3 Yr	5 Yr	10 Yr
Median Return	7.5%	8.4%	11.8%	8.9%	9.9%
Average Return	7.4%	8.6%	11.6%	8.8%	9.8%
Bond Indexes					
Midland Walwyn Index	7.1%	8.8%	12.1%	9.1%	
ScotiaMcLeod Universe	9.6%	10.9%	14.1%	10.9%	11.6%
ScotiaMcLeod Long Term	18.5%	16.3%	19.6%	14.1%	13.7%
ScotiaMcLeod Short Term	4.9%	7.8%	10.3%	8.5%	9.8%

There was about $21.5 billion invested in about 124 bond funds at the end of 1997, and the average MER for these funds was 1.59%. That represents fees of something in the order of $300 million every year.

Note that the average Canadian bond fund return is well behind the ScotiaMcLeod Universe index, a broad measure of the Canadian bond market, in each category. The long-term bond benchmark far outpaced the average bond fund, and even the short-term index matched the average fund's 10-year return.

Only four of 86 Canadian bond funds operating for at least five years were able to top the five-year 10.9% benchmark return. Only 14 were able to meet or exceed a five-year return of 10%, which is the average five-year return for the Midland Walwyn index and the ScotiaMcLeod Universe index combined.

Like Canadian equity fund MERs, bond fund MERs haven't been a big issue with investors partly because bond funds have produced great returns in recent years. Bonds have done well because interest rates have come down sharply. When interest rates fall, bond prices rise.

But now that interest rates are quite low, a 1.5% MER becomes much more important. In spring 1998, a long-term government of Canada bond (maturing in 25 years) was yielding about 5.8%. At that yield, a 1.5% bond-fund MER would chew up about 25% of your return.

BONDS AND INTEREST RATES

Bonds are very different animals from stocks. A stock can rise in value forever. A bond has a limited upside because a bond pays out a set amount of interest. The bond will rise in value if interest rates go down—but interest rates can't go to zero, so bonds can't rise forever.

Bonds have a yield and a price. The yield is roughly the annual return you will receive from a bond when you buy it, assuming you hold it until the bond matures. If interest rates rise, bond prices fall and their yields rise.

For example, if you buy a government of Canada bond when its yield is 6% and it matures in 10 years, you will receive a 6% annual return on your investment as long as you hold the bond until it matures and its principal is paid back. The only risk is that the government of Canada may for some reason be unable to pay you back your money, a highly unlikely occurrence.

You can buy traditional bonds that make regular interest payments, or zero-coupon "strip" bonds that don't make interest payments but gradually rise in value until they mature. Investors who want regular income buy traditional bonds. Long-term savers find strip bonds convenient.

Every weekday, bond traders sitting in the giant office towers of Toronto and other big cities furiously trade billions of dollars worth of bonds back and forth. The traders get up early in the morning to devour the day's economic data, talk to their firm's economists, and see how bonds in other markets are doing. They're all trying to figure out the same thing: Which way are interest rates headed?

A trader or fund manager usually sells a bond because he or she thinks interest rates are going up and that bond prices will fall. The buyers think interest rates are going down and that bond prices will go up. They can't both be right. For every winner there is a loser.

Over the course of a year, the winners among bond traders get fat bonuses from their firms, are written up in financial publications, and get invited to all the right parties. The losers keep their jobs—if they're lucky. The next year different people are declared the winners and losers. Meanwhile, the average return of actively managed bond mutual funds almost always lags a benchmark of bonds that aren't bought or sold. That's the effect of a 1 % or more MER, not to mention high levels of cash, on a bond fund.

The investor who buys a bond mutual fund is exposed to the bond-trading game, and to the significant fees charged by bond mutual funds. The lucky investor will wind up in a winning fund with juicy returns. More often, however, the bond mutual fund investor winds up in a fund that underperforms the average.

Most bond fund managers feel the need to speculate about interest rates, and they can't resist buying and selling bonds all day long in the belief that they know better than the next guy where interest rates are headed. The truth is that the direction of interest rates is incredibly difficult, if not impossible, to predict accurately.

If you have a big part of your savings in a bond fund, there is a real risk that your returns will substantially lag the bonds themselves. As we have already seen, a 1 % annual lag translates into a lot of money over years of saving.

Avoid these fees by buying your own bonds! Bonds issued by the various governments in Canada provide solid, dependable income at rates that are almost always higher than Guaranteed Income Certificates (GICs), with virtually no added risk.

BALANCED FUNDS

Another type of mutual fund is the balanced fund. This appeals to investors who want a highly diversified investment in one fund. Canadian balanced funds invest for the most part in Canadian stocks and bonds.

CANADIAN BALANCED FUNDS

	1 Yr	2 Yr	3 Yr	5 Yr	10 Yr
Median Return	11.0%	13.6%	14.3%	12.0%	9.8%
Average Return	11.2%	14.2%	14.6%	12.2%	9.7%
Bond Equity Indexes					
Midland Walwyn Index	7.1%	8.8%	12.1%	9.1%	
ScotiaMcLeod Universe	9.6%	10.9%	14.1%	10.9%	11.6%
TSE 300 Return	15.0%	21.5%	19.1%	17.5%	11.0%
Blended Index	11.7%	15.7%	16.1%	13.8%	11.3%

What shall we compare balanced funds with? Let's blend the five-year average bond benchmark of 10% with the TSE 300 return of 17.5% and get 13.8% for the five-year benchmark. The 10-year blended benchmark would be 11.3%. In both cases, the benchmarks are roughly 1.5% per year ahead of the mutual funds.

Canadians had about $45 billion invested in about 200 balanced funds at the end of 1997. These funds had an average MER of 2.1%, representing annual fees of something approaching $1 billion skimmed off by the mutual funds. You can avoid these fees by creating your own balanced portfolio of stocks and bonds!

MORTGAGE FUNDS

Mortgage funds invest mainly in residential mortgages. Mortgages are like bonds, but usually have lower returns. They're for the very risk-averse investor.

	1 Yr	2 Yr	3 Yr	5 Yr	10 Yr
Median Return	3.2%	5.7%	7.7%	6.8%	8.6%
Average Return	3.6%	5.9%	7.9%	6.9%	8.7%

Mortgages act like other fixed-income investments: They do well when interest rates are going down (as they have been in Canada for several years). Mortgage funds are great places to park small amounts of money for a short while, but they're unappealing for long-term investments. The average mortgage fund MER was 1.7% in 1997.

Why Stocks and Bonds are Better than Mutual Funds

The poor performance of Canadian mutual funds isn't the only reason why buying your own stocks and bonds is a better choice than mutual funds. Issues related to taxation, control of investments, education, and ethical considerations make do-it-yourself investing the better route.

Let's first understand just what a mutual fund is: a pool of money that belongs to many different investors. The sum is invested in various securities—stocks, bonds, and other investments—according to the fund's objectives.

Every mutual fund has a net asset value, which changes daily. This is the value of the fund's investments divided by the number of units, or shares, the fund has outstanding. The number of units changes all the time, as people put money into the fund and take money out.

Mutual funds make monthly, quarterly, or annual distributions, or payouts of interest income, dividends, and capital gains. Interest income is paid by bonds, treasury bills, mortgages, and the like. A capital gain is the profit earned from the sale of a security.

A dividend is a cash payout made by a stock. When a distribution is paid out to the fund's unitholders, the net asset value per unit of the fund drops by the amount of the distribution per unit. This is because money in the fund is being transferred to the fund's investors, and the net asset value of the fund must reflect this change.

As the value of the mutual fund's investments goes up and down, so does the net asset value of the fund.

UNFAIR TAXATION

Did you know that buying mutual funds can leave you with a tax bill on gains you didn't receive? It's another aspect of mutual funds that the fund companies rarely tell you about, but it happens frequently.

Let's say Bill puts $10,000 of non-RRSP savings into the Great Canadian Mutual Fund on Nov. 1, when the net asset value of the fund is $10.00. Assume the fund's investments then remain flat for the next two months. Let's say that during the year, sales of stocks in the Great Canadian have caused capital gains amounting to $1 per unit. On Dec. 31, the fund would distribute to its unitholders $1 per unit in capital gains, and the value of the fund would fall by $1 to $9.

See what happened? Bill was paid $1 in capital gains on which he must now pay taxes. The value of his fund hasn't gone up a penny, but he must now fork over money to the tax collector! Since Bill held 1,000 units of the fund, this means he must pay taxes on $1,000, or about $375 for people in the 50% tax bracket. Thanks for nothing, Great Canadian Mutual Fund!

A mutual fund's frequent stock trading can also trigger unwanted taxation. In the 1990s, the Altamira Equity Fund became famous for feverishly buying and selling stocks as if there were no tomorrow. This caused large capital-gains distributions to unitholders. For example, the fund paid $6.17 per unit in capital gains in 1993, when the net asset value finished the year at $28.14. Even though the Canadian stock market soared higher in the ensuing years, at the end of 1997 the Equity Fund's net asset value was actually lower—at $27.38, following significant payouts of capital gains every year since 1993. This type of trading by a mutual fund has no tax consequences if the fund is held inside an RRSP. But any investor holding this fund outside an RRSP would have forked over a sizable part of the fund's returns in capital-gains taxes during those years. That included a $3.31-per-unit capital-gains payout in 1997, when the fund's return was only 4.1%.

Of course, some mutual funds do practise the buy-and-hold strategy. But even buying and holding creates unfair taxation for investors who acquire the fund after its investments have already risen in value.

> **B**eware of buying established buy-and-hold funds outside your RRSP, warns Thomas Kingissepp, a chartered accountant and tax advisor with Ernst & Young in Toronto. Often, "you're buying this large accrued capital gain" in such funds, he says. When the fund eventually sells some of its bought-and-held stocks and distributes the significant capital gains, you'll have to dip into your other savings or sell another investment in order to pay the tax, Mr. Kingissepp notes.

Here's a hypothetical example:

The Fortune Teller Mutual Fund is launched in 1990, with only a dozen non-RSSP investors in it initially. The fund holds five stocks that are worth a combined one million dollars. The stocks do well, and after a few years the fund's solid performance figures begin to attract a surge of new investors into the fund. By 1997 the Fortune Teller has a thousand investors. There are now 50 stocks in the fund, but the original five stocks, still in the fund, are worth $5 million. The fund manager then decides to sell the original five stocks.

The same dozen early investors are still in the Fortune Teller. They have benefited from the full $4 million rise in the original five stocks, and this has been reflected in the net asset value of the fund. But the $4 million capital gain will be distributed to all the thousand investors in the Fortune Teller at the end of 1997! The original dozen are happy as clams, because the $4 million capital gain will be spread out to all of the thousand investors in the fund. The unwitting latecomers to the Fortune Teller fund will now pay capital-gains taxes on money they didn't earn. Holy unfair mutual fund capital-gains distribution method, Batman!

It's easy to find out how much potential capital-gains taxation you are exposing yourself to when researching a mutual fund. Take the fund's annual or quarterly financial statement, and compare the average cost of the fund's investments with their market value. You'll find these numbers at the bottom of the list of stocks that make up the fund. If there's quite a difference between the two numbers, then a significant undistributed capital gain rests within the fund.

The best way to avoid capital-gains taxes, fair or unfair, is to invest in stocks and bonds on your own, and hold them for as long as possible. We'll explore this in "Buy and Hold: The Smartest Approach."

THE HERD MENTALITY

A mutual fund's performance can be influenced by the behaviour of the people invested in the fund. Investors are attracted to mutual funds that have performed well. Similarly, investors tend to bail out of funds that don't perform well.

Mutual funds are supposed to be hands-off investment vehicles. But many investors find they must keep on top of the fund's performance and popularity to avoid the possibility of getting trampled by a stampede of exiting investors.

Sometimes the race for the exits can clobber a fund's performance. Exiting investors must be paid with cash from the fund, and the fund manager must sell stocks owned by the fund in order to raise the cash. This adds downward pressure to the stocks held in the fund, and can in turn reduce the value of the fund for the remaining investors.

To be sure, the stock market is full of investors who run for the exits at the first sign of trouble, whether or not they are in a mutual fund. But why carry an added risk of being in a mutual fund that experiences a massive outflow? It can seriously harm your returns.

DO YOUR INVESTMENTS
MATCH YOUR ETHICS?

All but a few Canadian mutual funds disregard any ethical standards for their investing. Most funds invest willy-nilly in whatever stocks the fund manager feels will provide good returns. If you invest in mutual funds, chances are you couldn't name more than a few of the investments in which you are participating. But many of us have ethical standards that we apply to everything we do in life, and we would like our investments to match our ethics.

For example, smoking is frowned upon by many Canadians today. It's clear that nicotine is addictive and that cigarettes cause health problems—even the tobacco companies admit this. Yet today's younger generation is full of smokers. Concerned investors may decide they don't want their money invested in cigarettes or tobacco-related products. In Canada, that means avoiding Imasco Ltd. (IMS-TSE), which owns Imperial Tobacco (Players and du Maurier cigarettes); and Rothmans Inc. (ROC-TSE), which makes cigarette brands such as Rothmans and Benson & Hedges. Many of the big Canadian mutual fund companies own Imasco, and it's also included in TIPS 35 (TIP-TSE) and TIPS 100 (HIP-TSE).

Certain resource-related companies may be off-limits for some investors' ethics. You may not favour forestry companies that chop down huge virgin forests, mining companies that chew up vast stretches of land to produce a few ounces of gold, industries that pollute our waters, or power companies that dam up pristine rivers. Few of us can claim we never use forest-related products, metals, or electricity, but we may still disagree with a particular company's practices and development plans.

Some investors may be concerned about pharmaceutical companies that make expensive drugs that are given to patients who may or may not need them. Alcohol, gambling, and companies that lend money or have significant debt loads may be no-nos for investors as well. Some people are avid public-transit supporters, and don't like cars. These people probably wouldn't want their money invested in any of the world's car companies or auto-parts suppliers. They would probably think twice about buying oil-company stocks as well.

Canada and the United States are chock-full of companies that operate in the industries mentioned above, and their stocks appear in many Canadian mutual funds and the popular stock indexes.

Ethical investing is a personal choice. We all have our own beefs about the way the world works. One person might admire the ability of Microsoft Corp. (MSFT-Nasdaq) to stave off the competition, but another might disagree with Microsoft's stranglehold on the computer software market. One person might despise the Canadian banks for not lending enough to small businesses, while another might find buying bank stocks an ideal way to recoup the banks' service charges through stock dividends.

No two people's ethics are exactly the same. That's why even investing in the few ethically oriented mutual funds available won't guarantee that your personal standards are being met. Do-it-yourself investing is the route to take for any ethically minded investor. In order to make stock picks that conform with your ethics, you'll have to have at least a general understanding of the companies you invest in. This is easily done and doesn't mean your investment returns have to suffer. Indeed, some ethical mutual funds have performed well because they've avoided resource stocks, which have been poor long-term performers.

DAY TRADING

A mutual fund's price, or net asset value, is determined at the end of every business day, by the last price paid that day for each of the stocks or bonds in the fund. When you request to purchase a mutual fund, your money goes to work the following morning, not the minute you put in your order. For mutual fund investors, it doesn't matter what the financial markets do during the day. It only matters where the market is at the end of the day.

Do-it-yourself investors, however, have an advantage because they can buy and sell on the spot whenever the market is open. If it isn't, the order to buy or sell will be executed when the market opens next.

Sometimes investors can benefit by not waiting until the end of the day. This includes times when the market is falling sharply. Once in a while, the stock market will nosedive in the morning, then come roaring back in the afternoon and close only slightly lower (or even higher) than the previous day. When markets are tanking, it's usually a great time to invest! To some people, this may seem illogical advice. But like any other purchase, stocks are better buys when they're on sale.

By no means should this suggest that you wait until markets are falling before you invest your idle cash. Remember, you invest in stocks because they go up over the long term, and very few people have displayed an ability to time the market. However, you might be driving in your car one day and hear on the radio that the stock market is sinking sharply. If you have idle cash, why not pull over and call in a buy order from a pay phone? Or on your lunch break you might notice a television report about a sudden market drop. If you have idle cash, this is a great time to put it to work.

Though day trading has its advantages, the key to successful investing is that you put your savings money to work as soon as you get it, not when you think it's a good time to invest. Waiting to invest usually leaves you in the dust while the market plows ahead. Remember, markets go up far more often than they go down. Don't let a sudden upswing or downswing in the market prevent you from investing.

WHAT ARE YOU LEARNING ABOUT BUSINESS FROM MUTUAL FUNDS?

If you own a mutual fund, you probably receive a seemingly endless stream of mail from the fund company. The literature tells you to invest early, invest often, stay the course, buy mutual funds, etc. There's often a letter from the fund manager or the fund company's president explaining why the stock market went up or down, how the economy is doing, which industries did well, how interest rates affected the market, or why stocks in Asia fell. Lately, these letters appear to contain an increasing number of explanations as to why the fund company's mutual funds had a bad year or fell behind the index, along with promises to improve the returns in the future. The tone of most of this literature is "Trust us. Just give us your money."

What's missing from all the pamphlets and letters is solid information about Canadian companies, what lines of business they're in, how they work, what their financial results are, and what their strategies are. Mutual fund companies rarely discuss individual stocks and companies in any detail, because they wouldn't want you to get too familiar with the names of companies in Canada and around the world. The fund companies don't want you to get the notion that you could buy these stocks on your own.

You don't get this information from mutual funds, but you do get it when you buy your own stocks. For one thing, most companies automatically mail their annual reports to their shareholders.

Further, the do-it-yourself investor gets to experience first-hand things like dividends paid by companies, stock splits, takeovers, and other company issues.

This doesn't mean it's necessary to follow a company in order to invest in its stock. Anyone can build and maintain a diversified investment portfolio without having to stay abreast of business developments. We've already seen that despite their business degrees and meetings with company executives, most mutual fund managers aren't able to keep up with the market averages. If you have absolutely no interest in business, you can, of course, still benefit from do-it-yourself investing. When you receive any annual reports in the mail, just make sure you plop them in the recycling box rather than the garbage.

But if you are interested in the world of business and want to learn more, you will find that investing on your own gives you a great grounding to learn all about business and finance. Maybe you think you're the next Warren Buffett, the Nebraskan who made billions by researching companies and simply buying and holding the right stocks over long periods of time. Or you might fancy yourself another Peter Lynch, who managed Fidelity's U.S. Magellan Fund with uncanny above-average consistency in the 1980s.

Chances are you won't be nearly as successful as these people. They're very rare birds. But there's no law that says a small investor cannot outperform most mutual funds. Indeed, you'll have a big edge by avoiding the annual MER. Doing your homework regularly to decide which stocks to buy and sell may or may not help to increase your returns further. Either way, learning about business can come in very handy if you start a company of your own one day, look for a new job, or find yourself chatting with the CEO of Humongous Industries Ltd. at a barbecue party.

INFORMATION SOURCES

The Information Age has opened up many different channels through which you can find out about companies and industry.

If you don't already have it, a subscription to a daily newspaper with a good business section is a top priority for the do-it-yourself investor who wants to learn about business. For Canadian business news, this means either *The Globe and Mail* or *The Financial Post*. The local papers in Canada's cities have a few pages devoted to business, but the information is usually geared towards local companies and is less than comprehensive about the national business scene.

For anyone buying Canadian stocks, a gem of a publication that many investors aren't even aware of is *The Toronto Stock Exchange Review ("The Review")*, published monthly by the TSE. *The Review* is packed with statistics on all the stocks traded on the TSE, including stock prices and movements, trading volumes, earnings per share, price-to-earnings ratios, dividends and dividend yields, number of shares outstanding, newly listed companies, and more. *The Review* also contains a detailed breakdown of the TSE 300, TSE 200, TSE 100, and Toronto 35 indexes, and the weightings of the stocks that make up those indexes. As we will discuss in detail later, the indexes laid out in *The Review* make an ideal guideline for a Canadian stock portfolio. You can purchase *The Review* in bookstores for as little as $13.

Other useful sources of business information for Canadians include monthly publications such as the *Canadian MoneySaver* (telephone: 613-352-7448), which is found in some magazine racks and offers stock-buying and tax strategies for penny-pinching savers. A one-year subscription is about twenty bucks. Call them up and ask for a free trial issue. *Canadian Business* is a monthly magazine with frequent articles on Canadian stocks and investment strategies. There's also a long list of investment newsletters that your discount broker can tell you about.

The Canadian Shareowners Association (telephone: 416-595-9600), headed by University of Windsor retired finance professor John Bart, offers various services for do-it-yourself investors. For a $76 annual fee, members can pay a $4 charge to invest small amounts of money (as little as $50) in a variety of well-known stocks, such as Royal Bank of Canada (RY-TSE), transportation concern Bombardier (BBD.B-TSE), entertainment giant Disney (DIS-NYSE), soft-drink king Coca-Cola (KO-NYSE), and McDonald's (MCD-NYSE). There were 43 stocks to choose from in the spring of 1998, including some index stocks, and the CSA is planning to add many more. The CSA also provides guidelines on how to analyze stocks. John Bart says it's easy for people investing on their own to make good stock picks. "The average guy can tell a great stock from a grief stock," he says.

The Internet is a growing source for business information. Much of the information you're looking for is somewhere on the Internet for free, but finding it can be time consuming. You'll find free stock quotes all over the place, but most are 15 minutes old. Live stock quotes are free over the phone or computer at most discount brokers anyway.

The Toronto Stock Exchange's website (www.tse.com) lets you monitor your own portfolio of stocks. *The Canadian Stock Market Reporter* (www.canstock.com) has corporate information for a monthly fee. Carlson On-Line Services (www.fin-info.com) offers free corporate information and company news releases.

Do-it-yourself investors also have at their disposal a daily barrage of business information about the United States, the current head office of the world's business.

For U.S. business news, *The Wall Street Journal ("Journal")* is your best bet, though a few *Journal* pages are included in the weekday *Globe and Mail*. The *Journal* provides broad coverage of big business in the U.S. and around the world like no other newspaper. *The New York Times* also has a good business section. The following magazines or weekly newspapers are also good for U.S. news: *Barron's, Business Week* (weekly magazine), *Forbes, Fortune, Smart Money,* and *The Economist. Value Line* is another U.S. publication packed with stats on companies and stocks.

For on-line business news, *The Wall Street Journal's* interactive edition is a popular and economical source at www.wsj.com or 1-800-369-2834 for information. The interactive edition includes the articles in *Barron's*. Dow Jones & Co., which publishes the *Journal*, also offers on-line information on thousands of companies. Ask your discount broker, check out http://djinterative.com, or call Dow Jones at 1-800-832-1234.

ANNUAL REPORTS

Once you've become a shareholder of a company, it will usually mail you a copy of its annual report a few months after the company's year end. (The year end could be in any month, not necessarily December.) An annual report is loaded with all kinds of information about the company's operations and financial track record. If the firm had a good year, you'll hear all about it. If it had a bad year, the CEO will usually try to explain why.

An annual report is a terrific source of information not only about the company that issued it, but about that entire industry. The annual report contains clues to help you decide about investing in the company and its industry. Consider the cover of Bank of Montreal's (BMO-TSE) fiscal 1997 annual report, which said in big letters: "Building Shareholder Value." This is the type of phrase you want to hear. Of course, merely declaring a commitment to shareholders doesn't ensure the stock will go up, but it does show you where management's priorities are. Bank of Montreal's commitment to shareholders was the driving force behind the company's plan to merge with Royal Bank of Canada (RY-TSE), as announced in early 1998.

The message from the CEO, president, or chairman at the front of most annual reports is a key source of information. Even the novice investor can get a feel for the company's management from this message. It's true that most firms tend to be openly bullish about their future, no matter what the circumstances are. Worthy companies back up their rosy outlooks with real figures and common-sense explanations of their business plans. They will also address any problems with their financial performance or business head on, and explain what steps are being taken to correct the situation. Read annual reports with a skeptical eye and look for promising outlooks supported by logical, understandable explanations.

You needn't rely on annual reports mailed to you by companies you already own. You can get just about any annual report free of charge. The cost is a phone call to the company's head office. Ask for investor relations or tell the operator you want an annual report. *The Globe and Mail* also has an annual report service at 1-800-965-6199 or www.icbinc.com, for any company with a club (as in the ace of clubs) beside its stock listing.

The financial statements are the meat and potatoes of any annual report. There are four:

1. the statement of income (or operations)
2. the statement of retained earnings (or the statement of changes in shareholders' equity)
3. the statement of cash flow (or the statement of changes in financial position)
4. the balance sheet.

Big established companies often include a five-year or 10-year summary of the highlights of the above statements, which is a very useful tool for the long-term investor.

Here are just a few basic questions to ask when perusing a company's financial statements in search of companies with steady long-term growth. Analysing a company's financial statements can be a wildly complex task, and companies in different industries are analysed in different ways. These are just a few things to look at to get a feel for a company's financial performance, but keep in mind that different industries require different analysis. And analysing a company's financial statements is by no means the sure road to making above-average investments for most investors.

- Statement of income: Did the revenues, operating income, and net income rise from the year before and previous years? Have the costs or expenses been rising less than the operating earnings in percentage terms? Were any "non-recurring, unusual, special, or one-time" charges or gains really that unusual?
- Statement of cash flow: Did the cash from operations or cash from operating activities rise from the year before and previous years? Is the company investing heavily? Did the company raise a lot of money from a debt issue or share issue?
- Balance Sheet/Retained Earnings: Are the assets mainly made up of tangible assets such as property, plant and equipment, and

cash? Or are they intangible entries such as goodwill and "other" assets? Did the shareholders' equity rise from the year before and previous years? Is the shareholders' equity substantially larger than the long-term debt?

The five-year or 10-year summary is perhaps an even better tool than the latest financial results for the long-term investor searching for quality companies. Here are some questions to ask:

- Is the long-term trend in earnings (or income) and earnings per share upward?
- Are the assets and shareholders' equity rising?
- Are costs or expenses and debt rising slower than revenues or operating earnings?
- Is the long-term cash flow trend upward?
- Is the long-term trend in earnings and shareholders' equity steady or erratic?

OR SHOW UP IN PERSON

Besides receiving annual reports, shareholders are also invited to attend a company's annual meeting. Most companies allow non-shareholders to attend as well. Annual meetings have a reputation for being dull, and many are. It appears that most shareholders go to annual meetings only to see what kind of spread the company sets out when the meeting's over. I've been to many annual meetings of companies running giant losses and whose share prices are tanking, and not a single shareholder asks a question. They just drift over to the food table when the meeting's over!

Most of us don't have the time to go to annual meetings anyway. But for those who do they're a great way to learn about business. Most companies are very good at putting a positive spin on the outlook for their business. If you go to annual meetings, leave your rose-coloured glasses at home and be highly skeptical of the company's presentation. Talk to the CEO afterwards if you want to. Common sense will help you decide if the company is worth investing in or not.

If you own a company through a mutual fund, you have no say in the issues and events that affect the company. Direct shareholders of companies get to vote (unless you own "non-voting" stock) on issues such as who's on the board of directors, how much the top management is being paid, and offers to acquire the company. Again, most of us don't have the time or interest to get involved in such matters.

For those who do have an interest in such issues, get involved! Make your voice heard at the annual meeting or in a vote. Companies don't change their ways unless they're under pressure to do so. For example, despite advances made by women in business in recent years, Canada's boards of directors include an appallingly low number of women. The only way to change this is to put pressure on companies at annual meetings or through letter-writing campaigns and the like. Very seldom does a mutual fund manager get up at an annual meeting in Canada to push for a company to change, so it's up to individuals and activist groups.

Self-Directed RRSPs and Non-RRSP Discount Broker Accounts

The Registered Retirement Savings Plan (RRSP) is one of the last remaining major tax breaks offered by the Canadian government for working Canadians.

The RRSP is a rockin' good savings tool that everyone should take maximum advantage of. The Self-Directed RRSP is an even better tool that has recently become affordable for even low-income Canadians.

An RRSP is a tax-sheltering investment vehicle that reduces your taxes and encourages you to save for retirement. You are allowed to make limited annual contributions to your RRSP; they are deductible from your income when you calculate your income tax. The current rules are that your RRSP contribution room for 1998 is 18% of your earned income in 1997, minus any pension adjustment, and subject to a limit of $14,500 in 1998 and $15,500 in 1999. Thereafter the limit will rise based on an index tracking Canada's average wages.

All income, dividends, and capital gains made from investments in your RRSP are untaxed as long as they remain in your RRSP. When you take money out of your RRSP, it is treated as income and taxed accordingly. An investment that is shielded from taxes experiences superior growth compared with taxed investments.

For this reason, it is imperative that you make every effort to contribute as much as possible to your RRSP. Make it your first priority for saving!

Many Canadians who aren't prodigious savers have misconceptions about RRSPs, and aren't aware of all the options. When some people say, "I'm thinking of buying an RRSP," they mean they're thinking of buying a Guaranteed Investment Certificate for their RRSP savings. These people often ignore their many other options.

THE CAN-CON RULES

An RRSP is a tax-sheltering vehicle, not an investment in itself. What you put in your RRSP is up to you, subject to some restrictions. The most common RRSP investments are cash, GICs, stocks, government bonds, Canada Savings Bonds, and mutual funds. According to current rules, at least 80% of the book value of your RRSP investments must be made with Canadian investments. (The book value is the amount paid for an investment, not what it's currently worth.)

A Canadian investment includes shares of Canadian companies, bonds and treasury bills issued by Canadian governments (federal and provincial) and Canadian companies, mutual funds that are fully RRSP eligible, Canadian cash, GICs, etc. Canadian companies are those that are registered in Canada, no matter where the company does business. For example, Seagram Co. (VO-TSE) is a Canadian company, even though the company operates worldwide and most of its top executives work in the United States.

IT'S YOUR CHOICE

The RRSP rules allow a lot of flexibility. For instance, you may carry forward unused RRSP room from previous years in order to contribute and deduct the combined amounts in the current year. Or you may decide to make an RRSP contribution one year, but not deduct it until a later year when your income is higher. This way, your investment grows untaxed and you minimize your income tax when it's most beneficial. You may even overcontribute up to $2,000 over your maximum deductible RRSP contribution in order to benefit from the tax-sheltered growth. An overcontribution isn't tax deductible until a future year when it may be deducted against any allowable RRSP room.

Few Canadians take advantage of the flexibility offered by an RRSP. Many investors are content buying GICs or mutual funds for their RRSPs instead of branching out into their own stocks and bonds. That's partly because financial advisors rarely counsel their clients to fill their RRSPs with their own stocks and bonds purchased at discount brokers. The advisors wouldn't make any money that way!

In order to buy stocks and bonds for your RRSP you must have a Self-Directed RRSP. This is an account that allows you to consolidate all of your RRSP investments into one account, and allows you to buy stocks and bonds as well as mutual funds, savings bonds, and GICs, and make other investments. If you don't already have a Self-Directed RRSP with a discount broker, it's now time to set one up, no matter how much money you have put away.

In the year you reach the age of 69, you must convert your RRSP into a Registered Retirement Income Fund (RRIF), purchase an annuity, or withdraw your RRSP money as income (and pay the required tax). If you want to manage your money, the best move here is to open a Self-Directed RRIF at a discount broker, which lets you buy and sell securities just as you do in a Self-Directed RRSP.

Many Canadians have investments all over town—GICs from three different banks, four different mutual funds, and a chequing account at a trust company. A Self-Directed RRSP eliminates this administrative hassle, since all of your investments are held in a single account with your discount broker. Your investments are consolidated on your account statements.

THE FALLING COST
OF SELF-DIRECTED ACCOUNTS

Today the banks and other financial-services companies are clamouring to win as many Self-Directed RRSP customers as possible. They know that every new customer they hook usually spells years of commissions and other business. As a result, the cost of operating a Self-Directed RRSP is plummeting and has become economical for even the most modest savings portfolios. It used to cost at least $100 per year to keep a Self-Directed RRSP account, even at the discount brokers. At several discount brokers today there's no charge for accounts with more than $15,000 or $25,000, and as little as $25 or so per year for smaller accounts. The fee is worth paying, even for investors just starting up.

Stock-trading commissions charged by discount brokers have dropped sharply in the last few years as they compete for the growing number of do-it-yourself investors. Bank of Montreal's Investor-Line was first out of the gate with the $25 flat rate for computer-based or automated telephone stock trades of up to 1,000 shares. That's the benchmark commission we're using in this book.

And discount brokers offer an ever-growing range of services, such as dividend re-investment plans for certain stocks, automatic monthly or quarterly withdrawal plans for RRSP contributions, margin accounts, short selling, and printed and electronic corporate information services.

The monthly or quarterly statements of clients' holdings give a detailed list of securities and cash held in the account, and any dividends or interest paid. These statements are getting better all the time. For example, many now show your RRSP's book value of Canadian investments, which makes it easy to max out the 20% foreign content. Some statements give warnings about upcoming maturing treasury bills or bonds. Stock quotes over the phone or computer are often free, or you're allowed thousands of them before a small charge kicks in.

THE DISCOUNT BROKERS

Below is a list of discount brokers that offer Self-Directed RRSP and non-RRSP accounts, and a few notes about their fees and services as of spring 1998. These fees tend to change frequently, so be sure to find out about fees and services before you choose your discount broker. Call up a few discount brokers or grab hold of their information packages and pick the one that best suits your needs.

Note that banking and brokering at the same financial institution can be convenient. This can allow you to buy and sell stocks and bonds from your savings account, without the hassle of writing cheques or making transfers from one institution to another. Also note that as of spring 1998 Bank of Montreal and Royal Bank were planning to merge, as were Toronto Dominion Bank and Canadian Imperial Bank of Commerce. The impact on their discount brokerage fees is unclear, but they'll probably go with the lower of the two.

Bank of Montreal—InvestorLine

(1-888-776-6886)

No annual fee for Self-Directed RRSPs containing more than $25,000. A $25 annual fee otherwise. Traditionally among lowest stock-trading commissions in the industry. Flat $25 commission for a stock trade of up to 1,000 shares done by computer or automated telephone system. US$25 for trading in U.S. stocks. Higher charges for orders done over the phone with a person.

Bank of Nova Scotia— Scotia Discount Brokerage

(Atlantic Canada 1-800-665-5559 / Quebec 1-800-361-6601 / Ontario 1-800-263-3430 / Manitoba, Saskatchewan, Alberta, N.W.T. 1-800-661-1955 / B.C., Yukon 1-800-561-3646)

No annual fee for Self-Directed RRSPs containing more than $15,000. A $75 annual fee otherwise. Commissions of $25 and up for Canadian stock trades and US$35 for U.S. stock trades done over the phone with a person. Discount of 20% for home computer trades.

Canada Trust—Market Partner

(1-800-560-6373)

No annual fee for Self-Directed RRSPs containing more than $50,000. A $100 fee otherwise. Commissions of $49 for stock trades valued up to $7,000, and a percentage charge for higher-value trades.

Less for computer trading. For U.S. trades, same commissions in U.S. dollars. Market Partner advertises "value-added trade execution," which it says can result in better prices for some trades.

Canadian Imperial Bank of Commerce— Investor's Edge

(1-800-567-3343)

No annual fee for Self-Directed RRSPs containing more than $15,000. A $100 annual fee otherwise. Minimum commission of $43 for stock trades in Canada, and US$43 for the U.S. when done over the phone, with a person. Savings of up to 25% for orders done through automated telephone service or home computer.

E*Trade Canada (a division of VERSUS Brokerage Services Inc.)

(1-888-283-7787)

Computer or phone trading commissions of $38.88 for up to 1,300 shares trading above $5 per share, and US$38.88 for U.S. stocks. A $38.88 annual fee for Self-Directed RRSPs. Company profiles and price charts free.

Hongkong Bank of Canada— Discount Trading Inc

(1-800-398-1180)

No annual fee for Self-Directed RRSPs containing more than $50,000. A $100 fee otherwise. Minimum commission of $40 for Canadian stock trades and US$40 for U.S. trades. Flat $29 commission for computer trading. Offers trading in several countries in Asia and Europe. Commissions are generally substantially higher than North American trading.

National Bank of Canada—InvesTel

(1-800-363-3511)

Commissions of $35 and up for Canadian stock trades and US$45 for U.S. stock trades. Lower commissions for computer trading. No fee for Self-Directed RRSPs.

Priority Brokerage

(1-888-597-9999)

Bills itself as a discount broker with "expert" staff. Commissions start at $50 for Canadian stock trades and US$50 for U.S. stock trades. Lower commissions for computer trading. A $50 annual Self-Directed RRSP fee, or no fee for active traders. Firm bought by major U.S. discount broker Charles Schwab.

Royal Bank of Canada—Action Direct

(1-800-769-2583)

No annual fee for Self-Directed RRSPs containing more than $25,000. A $25 annual fee otherwise. Flat $29 commission for home computer stock trades or $35 for automated telephone trades of up to 1,000 shares. For U.S. trades, same commission in U.S. dollars. Higher commissions for orders taken over the phone by a person.

Toronto Dominion Bank—Green Line

(1-800-465-5463)

Biggest of the discount brokers, as measured by number of clients. No annual fee for Self-Directed RRSPs containing more than $25,000. A $100 annual fee otherwise. Flat $29 commission for Internet stock trades or $35 for automated telephone trades of up to 1,000 shares. For U.S. trades, same commissions in U.S. dollars. Higher commission for orders done over the phone with a person. Offers stock trading in several countries in Europe and Asia. This costs far more in commissions. For example, the minimum commission for U.K. stocks is $150 for buy orders.

SWITCHING TO A DISCOUNT BROKER

RRSP investments made without a Self-Directed RRSP are registered at the mutual fund company, bank, or other financial institution where the investment was purchased.

> When you open a Self-Directed RRSP at a discount broker, you
> must request that all of your RRSP investments become reg-
> istered with the Self-Directed RRSP. Bring the latest statements for
> your RRSP investments to the bank or trust company where you
> want to open your discount broker Self-Directed account. Don't wait
> until the thick of RRSP season to switch your accounts to a discount
> broker or you'll be battling the masses in the banks.

The discount broker may outline some one-time fees that could
be charged to switch your accounts. During the RRSP season of
early 1998, many of the discount brokers were offering to waive
such fees, or rebate much of them. Take them up on these offers.

> Even if the discount broker isn't offering rebates, there's no harm
> in asking if they'd be willing to waive the fees in order to get
> your business. Many of them will say yes in a heartbeat, or at least
> give you a significant discount.

When you switch your RRSP investments to your discount broker Self-Directed RRSP account, ask to open a non-RRSP discount
broker account also, even if you don't have any extra money. As
fine a savings vehicle as the RRSP is, good savers know the importance of saving as much as possible outside the RRSP as well.

For those who are just starting out and don't have any money in
mutual funds or at a full-service broker, setting up discount-broker
accounts will be easy. For those who have decided to switch from a
mutual fund, full-service stockbroker, financial advisor, financial

planner, or similar advice giver, it's possible you will meet with resistance. Some may kick and scream when you tell them you're moving, and others will want to take you to lunch to set you straight. Some might downright beg you not to leave, and others might do their darndest to show you how badly you'll screw up if you start making your own investment decisions.

> Don't be talked out of your decision to switch to a discount broker! Maintain your resolve to take control of your own money. Managing your own money builds character, expands your knowledge of business and financial markets, has a big cost advantage over mutual funds, and is a whole lot of fun. And if you've been in an underperforming mutual fund for several years, don't get all mopy about your past results or the way you've managed your money. The past is past, and tomorrow's a new day! ⊙

Once you've switched your investments to your discount broker, it's time to do a little digging to find out what fees you're exposed to if you sell your mutual funds. If your investments include one or more mutual funds with declining sales charges, find out how far along the sales charge you are. For example, some funds have a sales charge of 5% that gradually declines to zero after five or seven years. The information is in the mutual fund's prospectus, if you've kept it. If not, you might have to phone the fund company.

With this information in hand for each of your funds, you must decide whether you can sell the fund without a charge or if you're willing to pay the charge in order to get out of the fund. You may decide that paying a one or two percent charge is worthwhile in order to get your money working for you in a low-fee manner. If you're on the hook for a 4% or 5% charge you may want to think twice before selling, but it's not crazy to sell anyway. It's a personal choice.

> **R**ead the fine print in your fund's prospectus. Some funds allow you to withdraw a certain amount of money per year with no sales charge. Also, there's no law against asking the fund company to waive the exit fee, especially if you've been with them for several years or if you've recently been switched into a different fund and the deferred sales charge has been reset. After all, you can explain to the fund company that they've already made good money from you on the MER the fund charges. Why not ask to speak to the Vice President of Whatchamacallit. Or write a letter to the president or chief executive officer of the fund company. Come on, Canada, let's do some complaining about high mutual fund expenses!

> **O**ne more word before we move on. Be kind to your discount broker. Don't call them up and ask if they think BigHuge Industries Inc. is a buy or not. Don't ask them to suggest some good computer stocks to buy or which utility stocks look good. Don't call them up when you're lonely and just want someone to talk to. And don't expect them to call you up to ask you how your daughter's violin lessons are going.

Discount brokers are mostly order takers. They'll help you with things like getting outside research on companies if you want it, or getting the highest-yielding government bond available. Their customer service folks will answer your questions about setting up accounts, how to buy and sell stocks and bonds, and what services they offer. But they aren't in the advice business.

This is why they're able to keep their fees low, especially if you use automated telephone trading or computer trading. The discount broker isn't your financial planner. You are the best financial planner you could have.

BUYING STOCKS THROUGH DISCOUNT BROKERS

If you don't know the lingo for buying stocks, it's best to learn a bit. Whether you're trading with your discount broker over the automated telephone system, by computer, or with a representative, the vocabulary is the same.

Computer trading and automated telephone trading usually cost much less than trading with a representative, so it's worthwhile to learn how. When you sign up with a discount broker, make sure to get a pamphlet that describes computer and automated telephone trading. Automated telephone trading involves following a series of recorded voice prompts to buy and sell stocks. Number combinations correspond with the letters of the alphabet, allowing you to get stock quotes or place buy and sell orders for the stocks you want, without actually talking to anyone.

When you open your discount broker accounts, you'll be asked to choose a password. Every time you make a trade, have your account number and password ready.

STOCK QUOTES

Just like a used car, a stock has a sticker price that you can pay. Or you can offer the seller something lower and see if you get a bite. Example of a stock quote.

	Bid	Size	Ask	Size	Last
TIPS 100 (HIP)	50.25	120	50.35	220	50.25

The "Ask" price for TIPS 100 here is the amount of money per share that people trying to sell the stock are asking. The "Bid" price is the amount of money per share the people trying to buy the stock are offering. The only way a trade will actually go through is when a buyer decides to pay the asking price, or a seller decides to receive the bid price. The "Last" price is the price last paid for TIPS 100.

The Size refers to how many "board lots" of stock are bidding at the bid price and how many are asking at the ask price. A board lot is 100 shares. In the above example, there are orders to sell 22,000 shares of TIPS 100 at a price of 50.35 per share, and there are orders to buy 12,000 shares of TIPS 100 at a price of 50.25.

> A traditional stock "quote" provides you with the Bid price and the Ask price. A "long quote" provides you with much more information, including the Size of the Bid and Ask, the volume of shares traded so far that day, the stock's high and low for the day, and the change from yesterday's closing price. You can get long quotes from discount brokers over the telephone or on your computer.

PLACING ORDERS

Let's say you call up or dial in to your discount broker looking to buy 100 shares of TIPS 100. You first enter your account number and password, then follow the menu prompts to place a "buy" order. You must always place a trade order with an instruction. The simplest instruction is "at the market," which means you purchase your stock at whatever the "Ask" price is.

> If you place your buy order at the market, then you'll be fairly certain to get your 100 shares for 50.35 per share. However, it's possible that the 50.35 asking price will change on you in the few seconds it takes to place your buy order. "At the market" is a perfectly good instruction for most investors, as long as the "spread" between the bid price and the ask price is small.

Rules governing TIPS 100 and TIPS 35 require that the spread is always 0.05 or 0.10 per share for these stocks. And most of the bigger Canadian companies have small spreads on their stocks. For smaller, less liquid stocks, however, sometimes the spread is significant. That's why it's important to get a stock quote before or while you're placing your order. If the spread on a stock you want to buy is between 0.05 and 0.20, then you're probably best off buying "at the market." That's because you'll be sure to get your order filled.

If the spread is larger, you might decide to set your Bid price. The advantage here is that you might get a better price for your stock than the Ask price. The disadvantage is that you might not get your stock at all if nobody's willing to sell it to you at your price. Setting your own price can involve many different types of orders, such as restricting purchases up to a certain price or keeping the order alive for a certain number of days. It will all be outlined in your discount broker material, but you'll probably find most of these different types of orders to be an unnecessary hassle.

Here's an example. Say you want to buy 100 shares of Maple Leaf Foods Inc. (MFI-TSE); the Ask price is 15.75 and the Bid price is 15.25. The size of the Ask is 5 board lots, and the size of the Bid is 25 board lots. You might decide to put in a buy order for 100 shares at 15.50. This way, you'll ensure you're first in line should anyone decide to sell Maple Leaf Foods at 15.50. When setting your own price, you must also indicate whether you're making a "day" order, which is only good for the day you make it, or some other type of order of longer duration.

After you've put in your buy order at 15.50, you'll need to find out later if your order was filled. This can be done by calling the discount broker back later in the day. Some of the discount brokers have or are working on automated "order status" systems that tell you if your trade went through. You can always speak to a representative at no charge. Some of the discount brokers also offer to call you when your trade goes through.

If your Maple Leaf Foods trade went through, you're in business. If it didn't, get a fresh quote and look at the Ask price. Did the Ask price move even higher, or did it get closer to your Bid? Are there a whole bunch more Bids at your Bid price? These are factors that might help you decide whether to make a different buy order or not.

> If you're going to change your buy order, be sure to call in and withdraw any existing buy order. You don't want to end up buying the stock twice.

When it comes to do-it-yourself investing, the last thing you want to do is spend all day trying to get the best possible price for your order. That's why "at the market" is the best instruction for most investors.

SETTLING TRADES

When you buy a stock, you have three business days to make sure there's enough cash in the appropriate account to cover the cost of the purchase and the commission. This means if you buy a stock for your RRSP, your RRSP account must have the required amount of cash in it. Likewise for non-RRSP accounts. Cash means cash—not money in a money-market mutual fund or a mortgage fund or a bond or whatever. Most discount brokers pay a reasonable interest rate on any uninvested cash that's sitting in one of your accounts.

If you buy a U.S. stock, you must make sure your account will cover the cost of the purchase, factoring in the exchange rate and any potential movements in the exchange rate over the three days. You may also decide to open a U.S. dollar account, but it isn't necessary. If you don't have enough cash in the appropriate account to cover your trade, you will be "offside," and liable for interest payments on the shortfall. You'll have to come up with the cash from somewhere else in order to cover the shortfall and "skate back onside."

The easiest way to ensure proper settlement of a trade is to make sure you have more than enough cash in the correct account before you call in your trade.

ODD LOTS

There's no law that says you have to buy in board lots of 100 shares! You can buy 50 shares, 10 shares, 125 shares, 275 shares, or even 1 share of a stock. However, because most stock trades are multiples of board lots, you might not always get the greatest price for your odd-lot order. It's a small price to pay for the long-term cost benefits of owning your own stocks directly, rather than through mutual funds. ⊙————

Here are a couple of examples. Microsoft Corp. (MSFT-NASDAQ) is a notoriously high-priced stock, meaning that its actual price has been in the $100 or higher range for many years. To buy a board lot of a $100 stock requires $10,000, not pocket change for small investors. Thankfully, you can buy 20 shares of Microsoft if you want, but you'll probably pay something like $101 per share, for a total purchase price of $2020 plus commission. Still, an extra dollar per share is no big deal for an investment that you plan to hold for many years.

An even higher-priced stock is Fairfax Financial Holdings Ltd. (FFH-TSE), which has traded as high as $600 per share. Not too many of us have $60,000 to be placing on a board lot of a single stock. That's why Fairfax often trades in odd lots. (Many investors have screamed for Fairfax to split its stock, to no avail.)

Don't let odd lots stop you from buying your own stocks, but do be careful of commissions. A good rule of thumb is to limit your commission to about 2% of the trade. With a commission of $25, that means you can spend $1,250 on a stock and still be at a 2% commission. Enjoy the fact that a typical Canadian mutual fund charges you 2% every year on your money, while a 2% commission on a stock you own for many years is a virtually negligible one-time fee. ⊙————

The Breakdown

WHAT PERCENT STOCKS, WHAT PERCENT BONDS?

Most investment advisors will tell you to hold a mixture of stocks and bonds for your savings. This is solid advice. The decision about your portfolio's breakdown between stocks and bonds, however, is yours to make.

An investment portfolio should be one thing above all else: diversified. A mixture of stocks and bonds will help ensure your investments are diversified. If your portfolio contains only stocks, you run the risk of a long bear market for stocks ruining your savings. If your portfolio contains only bonds, you run the risk of having returns that barely stay ahead of inflation.

Some investment gurus believe bonds are a total waste of time because stocks have done much better over long time periods. For example, according to an Investors Group report, Canadian stocks have returned about 10.7 % per year, on average, since 1950, while Canadian bonds have returned only 7.1 %. That's a huge difference when measured over the long term. U.S. stocks have provided even higher returns than Canadian stocks. Over the last decade or so in Canada, however, stocks and bonds have produced similar average annual returns—about 11 %.

Canadian stocks have soared over the past few years, which has led some to predict that they will cool off for a while. Still, many market-watchers argue that stocks are still likely to outperform bonds over the long haul. For one thing, bonds performed well over the last 10 years because interest rates dropped sharply. But interest rates can't fall forever, so the big returns posted by bonds in recent years are less likely to be repeated over the next several years.

Also, since the recession of the early 1990s, corporate Canada's focus on the bottom line has become more intense than perhaps ever before in the country's history. Stocks have never been more widely held and company managers are under greater pressure to provide good returns for shareholders and stock mutual funds.

But Canadian bonds could still continue providing good returns for several years. If Japan's experience in the 1990s is any indication of what may be in store for North American investors (and let's hope it's not), long-term bond yields could fall below 2 % while the stock market retreats for many years! In the 1990s, Japan's economy has been sluggish and its stock market has gone nowhere. Partly because there's been no inflation, Japanese long-term bond yields have fallen below 2 %, an incredible situation that nobody predicted during Japan's go-go 1980s. Canada has been in a virtually zero-inflation period for several years. This type of situation could make bonds a good place to be instead of stocks.

Of course, you can analyse the prospects of stocks versus bonds all you want, but you won't be able to determine which will be better investments over the next 10 or 25 years. The easiest way to avoid the stocks-versus-bonds guessing game is to own some of each!

WHAT IS A STOCK? WHAT IS A BOND?

Now let's examine just what a stock is and what a bond is, to help you make decisions about the portfolio breakdown that you're most comfortable with.

Companies issue common stock, or shares, to raise money to fund their operations. Big companies typically have many millions of shares outstanding. A share represents a part ownership of a company, or more specifically, part ownership of the equity of the company. That's why stocks are also called equities. A company's equity is its assets minus its liabilities. Shares generally rise in value over long periods of time as a company's earnings rise, which also increases its shareholders' equity and often leads to increased dividends.

A bond is an obligation for the bond issuer to pay interest on a principal sum of borrowed money, and to pay back the principal amount at a set time in the future (called the maturity date). A bond can be issued by a federal, provincial, or municipal government, a company, or an entity such as an airport or quasi-government agency. Canada Savings Bonds are more like GICs than bonds.

A bond has a price and a yield, which are constantly changing in the bond market. The price is the amount of money you must pay to own the bond, and the yield is the annual return you will receive if you buy the bond at its current price and hold it until maturity. The amount the bond pays in interest is set when the bond is first issued, and interest payments are made at regular intervals, such as every six months. The amount of these interest payments doesn't change.

The bond's price and yield are influenced by prevailing interest rates, the issuer's perceived ability to pay its obligations, and the time left until the bond matures. If interest rates are falling, bond prices rise and their yields will fall. That's because people are willing to pay more in order to secure the future flow of income. Conversely, when interest rates are rising, bond prices will fall and their yields will rise.

Government bonds are backed up by the government's ability to pay the interest and principal through taxation. Bonds issued by companies may or may not be backed up by the company's assets. Corporate bonds generally do not represent an interest in the company's equity or earnings. However, if a company goes out of business, the bondholders and other creditors will be paid off before the common shareholders.

PREFERRED SHARES

Preferred shares are another type of security, and they're usually more like bonds than stocks. Like bonds, investors buy preferred shares for regular income. While companies change their common-share dividend payout amounts frequently, a preferred share's dividends usually remain fixed. Preferred shares typically have a claim on the company's assets ahead of the common shares if the company becomes insolvent. If a company veers toward bankruptcy, its common shares can become worthless, but its preferred shares can retain much or all of their value.

Common shares usually carry votes for company issues, and preferred shares usually do not. Preferred shares are often callable, which means the issuer may opt to buy them back at a set price. And they may have other features, such as convertability into common shares. Investors seeking income outside the RRSP are attracted to preferred shares, since their dividends are taxed at a lower rate than interest payments from bonds. Like bonds, preferred shares tend to rise in value when interest rates fall, and vice versa.

STOCK AND BOND YIELDS

Bonds and stocks that pay dividends have a yield. A bond's yield is the annual percentage return the bondholder will earn at the price paid for the bond if it's held until maturity. An investor who buys a bond that matures in 2010 and that is currently yielding, say, 6%, will receive an average annual return of 6% if the bond is held until maturity. Such an investor shouldn't be concerned with the daily fluctuations of interest rates, for they have no effect on the investment as long as the bond isn't sold before maturity.

A stock's yield, known as the dividend yield, is much different. It is the expected or reported annual dividend per share as a percentage of its current stock price. When a stock price rises, its dividend yield falls. In this case, in order to increase the dividend yield, the company must increase its dividend.

Companies that traditionally pay decent dividends usually increase their dividend payouts when their earnings are rising. When companies perform poorly, they often cut their dividend payouts.

RISK

There's no limit to how high a stock can climb or for how long. A stock can also become worthless in a short period of time. A bond can rise in value as long as interest rates are falling, but interest rates can't fall to zero and so bonds can't rise forever. A bond's price will fluctuate but will eventually return to the principal amount or face value when the bond matures. A bond will only become worthless if the issuer becomes unable to pay the bond's interest and principal.

Bonds issued by the federal and provincial governments of Canada and by the U.S. federal government are considered virtually risk-free. The day-to-day prices of these bonds, therefore, are determined largely by movements of interest rates.

Because bonds issued by the various governments in Canada are considered safer than corporate bonds, government bonds usually have lower yields than corporate bonds.

Bonds issued by quality governments (such as Canada and the provinces) and quality companies are considered safer investments than common stocks. Bonds are also usually, but not always, less volatile than stocks. A stock can nosedive if a company releases bad news, or soar if there's good news. Bonds tend to move in gradual steps as interest rates trend higher or lower. And, it can't be repeated too often, a bond's fluctuating price is irrelevant to the investor who plans to hold the bond until maturity, as long as the issuer is able to repay the interest and principal.

FINDING YOUR BREAKDOWN

So which are better—stocks or bonds? If bonds provide guaranteed income, why would anybody take the risk of buying stocks? If stocks have consistently outperformed bonds in North America over the long term, are bonds really any "safer" than stocks? These are questions every investor must ask herself or himself.

What would you say to the following questions:

- Could you stomach losing some of your money from investing?
- Could you handle having an investment that stays flat for several years?
- Are you comfortable having investments that rise and fall in value quickly and frequently?
- Are you quite certain you won't need to spend your investments for several years?

If you answered with a strong "no" to these questions, then you should be mainly into government bonds. You're virtually guaranteed not to lose money this way. Do note, however, that an all-bond savings portfolio still has risk. It's possible that your returns will barely keep pace with inflation. There are, however, "real return bonds," which avoid this risk because they take inflation into account when paying you interest.

But if you can stomach periodic losses, you don't mind volatility in your investments, you're investing for the long term, and you're optimistic about the future of the world economy, then stocks should make up a healthy portion of your portfolio.

Generally speaking, the younger you are, the more risk you can afford to take. Your stock percentage should be higher. As you get older, it's wise to reduce your exposure to stocks since you could get caught in a nasty bear market just when you need the money.

Here are a few breakdown scenarios for a savings portfolio. This is roughly the advice given out by Canadian financial institutions, the Canadian Securities Course, and many financial planners. Note that there's no allotment for cash. Most advisors also recommend keeping some cash on hand for emergencies and the like. That's just common sense.

Age: Mid-twenties. Steady income. Saving for house and retirement. No dependants.

Stocks: 60%-90%
Bonds: 10%-40%

Age: Late thirties. Higher income. Mortgage. Two kids. .

Stocks 60%-90%
Bonds: 10%-40%

Age: Pushing 50. Entering peak earning years. Paying down the mortgage. Kids entering university.

Stocks: 40%-70%
Bonds: 30%-60%
(When you get into your 50s, start to avoid buying bonds with long maturities, such as 25 or 30 years.)

Age: 65 and up. Retirement. House paid off. Kids fending for themselves.

Stocks: 0%-40%
Bonds: 60%-100%

Again, this is only a rough guideline. The final decision about your stock-to-bond breakdown is best made for yourself, taking into account your income, your tolerance for risk, your expenses, your need for steady investment income, etc. Common sense will guide you.

RRSP STRATEGY: WHAT'S IN, WHAT'S OUT

Once you've decided how much of your savings should be in bonds and how much in stocks, another important decision is which investments to hold in your Self-Directed RRSP, and which to hold outside. This decision is all about avoiding Revenue Canada's clutches.

For many Canadians the RRSP strategy is simple because they don't have any savings other than their RRSP. Their breakdown, then, should be made within the RRSP.

How Investments are Taxed

Let's take a look at how the various types of investments are taxed.

Money contributed to an RRSP can be deducted from income and then grows tax-free until removed from the RRSP. Money removed from an RRSP is taxed as income, no matter how the money was invested.

Money invested outside an RRSP is a whole different ballgame. There are three main types of investment income:

1. interest

2. dividends

3. capital gains.

Generally speaking, full taxation applies to interest, while only 75% of capital gains are taxed. Dividend income from Canadian companies is also taxed at a lower rate than interest income; a tax credit equal to roughly 25% of the dividend applies. Interest income and dividends from foreign sources are treated as income for Canadian tax purposes, while capital gains on foreign investments are taxed the same as capital gains on Canadian investments.

Interest income is paid by bank accounts, treasury bills (bonds that mature in less than a year), GICs, savings bonds, government and corporate bonds, and the like.

A capital gain is the difference between what you paid for a security and the amount you received upon selling it. If this number is negative, then it's a capital loss. All capital gains incurred in a year, offset by any capital losses, make your net capital gain (or loss). Only 75% of the net capital gain is taxed. Similarly, 75% of any net capital loss may be used to offset taxable capital gains in future years or for up to three previous years.

Dividends paid by shares of Canadian companies are taxed differently. You must "gross up" the amount of the dividend by 25% for tax purposes, and this becomes your taxable dividend income.

Then you receive a federal dividend tax credit that represents roughly 25% of the dividend you received once federal and provincial taxes are factored in.

WHAT GOES IN?

There's much debate about what investments to hold in your RRSP and which to hold outside. But one thing is clear: Bonds and other interest-paying investments are better off inside your RRSP, since the income is sheltered from otherwise full taxation. Of course, if you're a bond-only investor then you'll probably wind up owning some bonds outside your RRSP as well.

But an RRSP full of bonds stands a low chance of ever becoming the small fortune that many younger working Canadians dream about having for retirement. That's why you should consider having at least a modest portion of your RRSP in stocks.

Young or middle-aged folks can afford to load up their RRSPs with stock investments. Though you technically lose the favourable tax treatment of dividends and capital gains earned outside an RRSP, such benefits can't hold a candle to the benefits of tax-sheltered growth over many years.

A younger person's RRSP stock portfolio can be switched over to bonds later in life as retirement approaches, without triggering any taxation.

WHICH STOCKS IN, WHICH STOCKS OUT

Some stocks make better sense than others for inside an RRSP. For example, common stocks that pay good dividends are well suited for an RRSP because the dividends won't be taxed, nor will the capital gain upon selling. And these stocks tend to be relatively low-risk utilities such as phone companies or power companies, banks and other financial institutions, and pipeline operators. These are often called "interest-sensitive" stocks, since their prices are affected by interest rates as well as corporate developments.

Other good RRSP candidates are stocks that you don't necessarily plan to hold for the long term. That's because you won't get dinged with a capital-gains tax bill when you sell the stock in favour of another security.

Preferred shares can work inside your RRSP, but only if you've checked that your dividend yield is better than the yield on government bonds at the time of investment. Since the favourable tax treatment of dividends doesn't apply to RRSP investments, pre-tax yield is everything when deciding between preferred shares and bonds for an RRSP.

Preferred shares often make sense outside your RRSP if what you're looking for is secure, steady income with a good tax break, and you're not trying to hit any home runs. When selecting preferred shares, security is a high priority. It's best to stick with the banks, phone companies, and utilities, most of which have preferred shares that are part of the newspaper's stock listings. There are also preferred "split" shares, some of which offer diversity in a single stock (see "The Gambler"). When choosing a preferred share, it's a good idea to call the issuing company to get details. Many preferred shares have terms that allow the company to buy them back at a set price, or convert them into common shares. Sometimes preferred shares have so many terms and conditions that they're not worth getting into.

The one type of stock investment that's best done outside the RRSP is the mega-long-term buy-and-hold stock. This is your extra savings on top of your RRSP savings (if you can manage it!) that you're setting aside also for retirement, for that first-class round-the-world trip you're planning to take when you get older, that 22-foot sailboat, or that country home or cottage you've always wanted to have when you retire.

The deal here is that you make an investment or two outside the RRSP, and you have no intention of selling it until it buys you your dream purchase or when you need the money come retirement. The proceeds from the eventual sale will benefit from the capital-gains tax break rather than be taxed as income when removed from the RRSP. This strategy should be reserved for the bluest of the blue-chip stocks, or perhaps even better, one of the index stocks that we'll discuss in a later chapter. Buying an index stock outside the RRSP is a great way to add to RRSP savings in a tax-efficient way. That's because, unlike mutual funds, these stocks pay little or nothing in capital-gains distributions and pay only modest dividends. Index stocks are also diversified investments that outperform most mutual funds and cost far less in annual expenses.

Buy and Hold

THE SMARTEST APPROACH

Speaking of mega-long-term investing, let's look at the buy-and-hold approach to investing. As you map out your breakdown and decide what's in and what's out of your RRSP, keep in mind the big advantages of buy and hold.

Buy and hold is an investment concept aimed at maximizing returns, partly by avoiding taxation and fees. Several mutual funds claim to have a buy-and-hold investment approach. But as we've seen, most funds cause unfair capital-gains taxation and charge significant MERs, which means they're not really applying the buy-and-hold philosophy. The only true way to buy and hold is to invest on your own.

Buy and hold is a method of investing that's been popularized by successful investors such as Warren Buffett, the U.S. billionaire. Buffett's trick is buying stocks of companies with great growth potential for the long term, which can mean several decades. For example, a few decades ago he bought a big chunk of Coca-Cola Co. (KO-NYSE) and sat back while his investment multiplied many times over the years. Sound simple? It is, as long as there's still good reason to hold on to the stock. Coca-Cola's stock has been a stellar perfomer for years; partly because its products can be sold anywhere to anyone. Other Buffett picks include or have included Gillette (G-NYSE), American Express (AXP-NYSE), McDonald's (MCD-NYSE), and U.S. government bonds. His investments are held in a company called Berkshire Hathaway (BRKB-NYSE), which is also traded on the New York Stock Exchange.

By buying a stock or a stock-market average and not selling it, you avoid getting stuck with frequent capital-gains tax bills that reduce your returns. Second, buying and holding keeps you from being tempted to try to beat the odds and outsmart the stock market. Third, buying and holding keeps commissions to a bare minimum.

DON'T TIME THE MARKET

Buy and hold means you plan to own the stock or the index stock for many years. It means you don't panic and sell when your investment goes down 15% a few weeks or a year after you bought it. Buy and hold means you don't fret if your investment stands still, even for a few years. It also means not being tempted to sell winning investments.

People buy stocks because they tend to go up over long periods of time. Some go up steadily year after year. Some do nothing for several years then surge higher. BCE Inc. (BCE-TSE), for example, went nowhere for years on end before rocketing higher in the mid-1990s. Some stocks go way up and then way down but appreciate over the long term. Sometimes the entire market moves in these ways.

Stock-market averages have trended higher for generations, but few professional investors are happy with the average. That's why they rely on in-depth research before buying a stock. That's why they watch the stocks they own like a hawk. That's why they buy and sell frequently, often the same security in a single day. And on and on.

Everyone who sells an investment has a reason for doing so: The stock became overvalued; the company lost its focus; my broker told me to sell, the stock has already doubled or tripled. Sometimes the investor will be right and the stock will go down. But, because the market goes up more often than it goes down, the speculator who sells a stock will be wrong more often than right.

To be sure, the stock market can spend years on end not going anywhere. The Dow Jones Industrial Average spent most of the time from 1965 to about 1982 trying to move up past 1,000, an excruciating time for anyone holding stocks through those years. Nobody could have predicted that stocks would move sideways for so long.

And certainly nobody predicted what happened next. The period from the early 1980s to the late 1990s marked the greatest bull market (period of rising stock prices) of all time in U.S. stock-market history. The Dow Jones Industrial Average went from around 1,000 to 9,000 by summer 1998. Yet it seemed that nearly every month during this huge run-up in stock prices, somewhere in the major business media appeared an article or a commentary about how ridiculously high stock prices were, and how they were about to tumble.

Sure, stocks were expensive by some historical measures at various times during this big run-up. But the point is, despite howling protests by legions of "professional" investors and learned commentators, the stock market marched steadily higher. Anyone who got cold feet missed out on some fabulous returns. Can you imagine telling someone in 1982, after about a decade and a half of flat stock prices, that the stock market would be nine times higher in roughly another 15 years? They'd have put you in a straitjacket.

By the late 1990s many commentators were using the words "mania" and "speculative bubble" to describe the lofty valuations on the U.S. stock market. The problem is, these terms were used to describe the stock market in 1995, 1996, and 1997, a period when the Canadian stock market rose about 70% and the U.S. stock market more than doubled! Even if a bear market (period of falling stock prices) were to arrive, it would have to be a nasty one indeed to erase just those three years of stock-market appreciation.

A GOOD, LONG RUN

Yes, valuations on North American and European stock markets will come down one day, if they haven't already. It could be through a spectacular stock-market plunge, a slow downward crawl, or another long sideways move while corporate earnings catch up with the companies' stock prices.

The $6 trillion question is when? And the answer: Nobody knows. So why fight it? Buy-and-hold investors enjoy the ups and suffer through the downs but have faith in the long term, especially when they're diversified internationally.

Buying and holding a country's stock index can be done for decades. Sometimes it takes a lot longer than we would like, as with the U.S. stock market in the 1970s. And it's been no fun at all for anybody invested in the Japanese stock market in the 1990s. Eight years after Japan's stock market fell by more than half, the market was no higher. Such is the nasty after-effect of the kind of speculative bubble Japan's stock and real estate markets experienced in the 1980s.

Buying an individual stock, on the other hand, doesn't mean you stubbornly hold on to it forever, no matter what happens. There are times to sell, which we will explore shortly. The most obvious time, for example, is when you need the money. But buying and holding works very well, for the most part, with individual stocks of big, established multinational companies.

Let's look at an example that shows the tax benefits of buying and holding.

Sammy buys 100 shares of XYZ Corp. outside his RRSP at $10 per share, for a total investment of $1,000. (We'll leave commissions out to keep things simple.) In three weeks the stock rises to $12 and Sammy figures he's made a good profit, so he cashes out. Sammy now has $1,200, but must cough up, say, 40% in capital-gains taxes on his $200 profit, or $80 in taxes. Over the following week, Sammy has trouble finding another suitable investment, and a positive article about XYZ Corp. makes him decide to get back in. He buys 100 shares of XYZ Corp. and gets in at the same price he sold at, $12 per share, or $1,200. Sammy is now back to owning 100 shares of XYZ Corp., but must come up with an extra $80 to complete his purchase.

Even if Sammy had gotten back into XYZ Corp. for less than $12, it still could have been a bad move to sell in the first place. In fact, for his sale and repurchase of XYZ Corp. to make sense, Sammy would have had to get back in to XYZ Corp. at a price lower than $11.20 per share, in light of his $80 tax bill. Selling a stock and buying it back cheaper afterwards isn't easily done, and it's a lot more like gambling than investing.

If you try this outside your RRSP the tax collector will be a big obstacle to your success. And your next investment will have to earn a significantly higher return than the one you just sold in order for your move to make sense. Even inside the RRSP the odds are against you for quality stocks. If the stock market generally moves forward most of the time, then it follows that the odds of correctly timing the downturns of any individual stock are against you. Need we mention the added harm to investment returns that commissions cause?

DIVIDEND REINVESTMENT PLANS

A convenient method of buying and holding a stock is to use the DRIP feature. This stands for dividend re-investment plan, and many big Canadian companies offer DRIPs for their stocks. The deal is you buy a few shares of a DRIP-eligible stock through a discount broker, and instead of receiving your dividends in cash, they automatically go toward buying more shares of the company with no brokerage charge. It's a very handy feature that ensures your dividends are going to work for you, cost effectively, the minute they're paid.

There used to be a cumbersome process of buying DRIP stocks, which involved getting hold of the actual share certificate of a company you bought and registering your shareholding with the company. But today the discount brokers take care of most of the work if you request the DRIP feature. And the number of DRIP stocks is growing all the time. For example, below is a list of some of the DRIPs that Bank of Montreal's InvestorLine was offering as of spring 1998:

- AGRA Inc. (AGR-TSE)
- Alcan Aluminium Ltd. (AL-TSE)
- BC Telecom Inc. (BCT-TSE)
- BCE Inc. (B-TSE)
- Bank of Montreal (BMO-TSE)
- Bank of Nova Scotia (BNS-TSE)
- CAE Inc. (CAE-TSE)
- Canadian Tire Corp. (CTR.A-TSE)
- Canwest Global Communications Corp. (CGS.S-TSE)
- CT Financial Services Inc. (CSA.A-TSE)
- Canadian Pacific Ltd. (CP-TSE)
- Fortis Inc. (FTS-TSE)
- Imasco Ltd. (IMS-TSE)
- Imperial Oil Ltd. (IMO-TSE)
- Inco Ltd. (N-TSE)
- MacMillan Bloedel Ltd. (MB-TSE)
- National Bank (NA-TSE)
- Northern Telecom Ltd. (NTL-TSE)
- Nova Scotia Power Inc. (NSI-TSE)
- TransCanada PipeLines Ltd. (TRP-TSE)
- Westcoast Energy Inc. (W-TSE).

WHY BUY-AND-HOLD FUNDS DON'T WORK

We've already seen how funds that make long-term investments create unfair taxation. We've also seen how funds that trade frequently create excessive taxation.

Another reason that buy-and-hold mutual funds don't make sense is that they defeat one of the purposes of "buy and hold," which is keeping fees to a minimum. Let's take a peek at a real live Canadian mutual fund that bills itself as a buy-and-hold fund. The Infinity Canadian Fund's literature states: "We believe that owning a portfolio of excellent businesses, domiciled in strong long-term growth industries, represents your best opportunity for capital appreciation over time." The literature then goes on to underscore the tax advantages of buy and hold.

Too true, but when you dig into the fund's prospectus you find a major drawback with the strategy when it's done in this mutual fund—a management expense ratio of 2.95%!

A 2.95% MER is very high, even by Canadian mutual fund standards, and acts as a major drag on long-term returns. If the stocks in such a fund were to return, say, 12% a year for 25 years (an aggressive assumption), they would turn an initial investment of $25,000 into $425,003. With a 2.95% MER, however, the fund's investors would receive only $218,063. Yikes.

In early 1998, the Infinity Canadian Fund included 25 Canadian stocks and 10 U.S. stocks. To buy these stocks yourself would cost about $1,000 or so in discount-broker commissions. Sound like a lot? At a 12% even annual return, your stocks would be ahead of the fund after less than two years, even after the $1,000 in commissions was deducted from the initial $25,000 investment. That's because after the MER is factored in, the fund's returns become only about 9% per year.

Having made these points, the Infinity Canadian Fund contains some interesting stock picks (listed below) that have been performing quite well. Note, however, that the fund is heavy with mutual fund company stocks. If the growth of the Canadian mutual fund industry levels off, then mutual fund company picks might not be so great for the long term.

Here are the fund's stocks. You might want to buy a few or all of them for your own buy-and-hold portfolio!

CANADA

- AGF Management (AGF.B-TSE) — mutual funds
- Bank of Montreal (BMO-TSE) — bank
- Bank of Nova Scotia (BNS-TSE) — bank
- Bombardier (BBD.B-TSE) — planes, trains, jet skis, etc.
- BPI Financial (BPF-TSE) — mutual funds
- CanWest Global Communications (CGS.S-TSE) — TV broadcasting
- Canadian Imperial Bank of Commerce (CM-TSE) — bank
- Dundee Bancorp (DBC.A-TSE) — mutual funds
- Fairfax Financial (FFH-TSE) — insurance
- Franco Nevada Mining (FN-TSE) — gold mine royalties
- Kingsway Financial (KFS-TSE) — insurance
- Loblaw (L-TSE) — supermarkets
- Loewen Group (LWN-TSE) — funeral homes
- Mackenzie Financial (MKF-TSE) — mutual funds, financial services
- Magna International (MG.A-TSE) — auto parts
- MDS Inc. (MHG.B-TSE) — health care technology
- Milltronics (MLS-TSE) — industrial measuring equipment
- Montrusco Associates (MTA-TSE) — financial services
- Newcourt Credit Group (NCT-TSE) — non-bank lending
- Power Financial (PWF-TSE) — mutual funds, insurance
- Royal Bank (RY-TSE) — bank
- Sceptre Investment Counsel (SZ.A-TSE) — mutual funds
- Thomson Corp. (TOC-TSE) — publishing and information services
- Toronto Dominion Bank (TD-TSE) — bank
- Trimark Financial (TMF-TSE) — mutual funds

UNITED STATES

- Aetna Inc. (AET-NYSE) — insurance, employee services
- American Express (AXP-NYSE) — credit cards, financial services
- Berkshire Hathaway (BRKB-NYSE) — Warren Buffett's stock picks
- Coca-Cola (KO-NYSE) — beverage giant
- Gillette (G-NYSE) — shaving products
- Johnson & Johnson (JNJ-NYSE) — health care products
- Microsoft (MSFT-NASDAQ) — computer software king
- Procter & Gamble (PG-NYSE) — consumer products
- Walt Disney (DIS-NYSE) — entertainment giant
- Wells Fargo (WFC-NYSE) — bank

A TIME TO SELL

Welcome to the most difficult section of the book. When to sell a stock?

This is a question that every investor wrestles with and never really knows the answer to. It doesn't matter whether you're a mutual fund manager, a do-it-yourselfer, or Warren Buffett or Peter Lynch.

One of the major advantages of index stocks over individual stocks is that you never need worry about selling an index stock, and the people who manage the index stocks do all the buying and selling of stocks that make up your index stock.

Individual stock investors, however, do have to ponder selling their investments. Ideally, you don't sell any of your stocks until you're retired because they all keep going up. Unfortunately, this isn't likely to happen and there's no way to know for sure when the right time to sell is.

Some investors have a policy of selling any stock that falls 20% or more after they've bought it. Some sell when a certain price target is reached. Some buy stocks with low P/E ratios and sell them when the P/E ratio becomes high. Who's to know?

The streets are strewn with investors who chickened out of the stocks of the Canadian banks, pipelines, phone companies, and others after they doubled in the mid-1990s, only to watch those stocks surge higher and sometimes double again. And the streets will be strewn with investors kicking themselves for buying these stocks right at their peaks before they pull back or go sideways for a few years, whenever that turns out to be.

Countless analysts and fund managers pronounced an end to Coca-Cola Co.'s (KO-NYSE) awesome growth at various times in the 1980s and 1990s, only to watch Coke extend its international reach and command an ever-higher stock price. Countless investors balked at the high P/E ratios of Microsoft Corp. (MSFT-NASDAQ), Dell Computer Corp. (DELL-NASDAQ), and Walt Disney Corp. (DIS-NYSE) during the 1990s, even as these stocks marched relentlessly upward. And countless other investors will rue the day they bought these stocks when and if they ever go down for a long time.

Don't let the question of when to sell a stock consume your thoughts. Do-it-yourselfers need only address the question of when to sell once a year during their annual investment portfolio checkup. More hands-on do-it-yourselfers might want to ask the question more often, but it's not necessary. Remember that if your Canadian stocks are still in the TSE 300 then the index hasn't sold your stock.

Here are a few reasons not to sell a stock for the long-term investor.

1. I've already doubled, tripled, or quadrupled my money.

2. The stock market is down, and so are my stocks.

3. I read that so and so sold the stock or says it's time to sell.

4. It's been a few years and the stock hasn't gone up.

REASONS TO SELL

And here are a few straightforward reasons why you would sell all or part of a stock.

1. I need the money.
2. The stock got kicked out of the TSE 300.
3. The stock nosedived or is now a penny stock.
4. The stock accounts for more than 25% of my savings.

> **N**eeding the money is the best reason to sell a stock. If you have to choose between holding a stock and taking a trip to Spain, go to Spain. Going to Spain is more fun than owning a stock. You can't work on your tan or your Spanish with a stock, and Spanish food is far tastier than any stock. And if you get run over by a truck one day, owning a stock won't do you any good but at least you will have been to Spain.

When it comes to Canadian stocks, one strategy is to sell a stock if it gets kicked out of the TSE 300. Remember that it's the TSE 300 index that outperforms most mutual funds, so why hang on to a stock that can't keep up with the TSE 300?

This doesn't mean you have to be constantly checking to see if your stocks are still in the TSE 300. A stock doesn't fall to zero just because it got kicked out of the index, though some stocks have done just that before the index had a chance to give it the boot. Get a copy of *The Toronto Stock Exchange Review* for your annual portfolio checkup and look to see if your stocks are still in the TSE 300 index. Sell any stocks that have dropped out. Again, you might decide to set a different cut-off point for your stocks—such as selling any stock that falls below a 0.05% weighting in the TSE 300, for example, or holding only stocks in the TSE 100.

STOCKS THAT NOSEDIVE

> Stocks that nosedive are also usually good ones to sell. Again, this doesn't mean you have to monitor their every move. Stocks that nosedive often do so in a very short time period anyway, as in a few seconds or days, so only a few lucky investors are able to get out before it's too late. It's no fun to own a stock that nosedives, but take some twisted sense of comfort from the fact that it happens to everybody. It happens to the mutual funds, it happens to the indexes and the index stocks, and it could very well happen to you. That's why you must be certain that your portfolio is highly diversified.

A nosedive is a stock that goes from $35 to $6.00, $7 to $0.85, $65 to $12, or something along those lines while you own it. A stock that nosedives is like an airplane spiralling down on fire. Something has gone terribly wrong, and the best chance you have of saving yourself is to bail out. "Nosedive" also refers to stocks that have become penny stocks, which are stocks that trade under $5.00 a share. The fact is, when you pore over the stock pages, it's the penny stocks that are the most speculative or belong to second-rate companies.

Of course, nosedive stocks sometimes manage to pull up at the last second and gain altitude again. Everybody wrote off steelmaker Stelco Ltd. (STE.A-TSE) as a goner at about 75 cents a share while the recession dragged on in the early 1990s. But Stelco survived and the stock was back to $12 a few years later, a nice score for those who kept the faith. (The stock is still well below its 1983 high of about $30, however.) And everybody was cocksure that Magna International Inc. (MG.A-TSE) was on its deathbed in the late 1980s and early 1990s, ravaged by a high debtload and overcapacity in its plants. However, the company was successfully resuscitated by a team of top financial doctors. Magna surged from a low of about $2 per share to $60 in a few short years, and today thrives as one of the world's biggest auto-parts companies. Again, a tasty gamble for anyone who took it. But who knew?

> The reason that selling the nosedive stocks makes sense is that for every Magna or Stelco there are about two or three nosedive stocks that go completely off the radar screen or spend years flying dangerously close to the ground never to regain altitude.

Remember the real-estate washout of the early '90s? Several big names such as Campeau Corp., Bramalea Ltd., and Olympia & York (a private company) bit the dust, even while many commentators were assuring us that the good times were just around the corner. Bad real-estate loans sent shares of Royal Trustco Inc. nosediving as well, before a big chunk of the company's assets were bought by Royal Bank of Canada.

Canada's high-tech industry is littered with the wreckage of failed companies that appeared to be so promising in their heydays. Remember Gandalf Technologies Inc.? Many professional investors hung on until the bitter end. Same with Tee-Comm Communications Corp., the home TV satellite company. Some other names that flamed out: Incontext Systems Inc., Hookup Communication Corp., Fulcrum Technologies Inc.

Another nosedive was Philip Services Corp. (PHV-TSE), a stock that had quickly risen to about $28 in mid-1997, only to slide to about $3 by the summer of 1998. Philip, an industrial services and recycling concern, shocked investors with a string of bad news. The company said millions of dollars' worth of copper had gone unaccounted for, causing the company to take big writedowns against its earnings and restate its previously reported earnings. It will be interesting to see if the stock ever regains its former glory.

There's a very long list of Canadian mining stocks that have crashed and burned, or spent years on end going nowhere. Several forest-products stocks have also been dead money for many years.

Some other stocks that nosedived and haven't rebounded to anywhere near their pre-crash levels after many years include Canadian Airlines Corp. (CA-TSE), Cineplex Odeon Corp., private-label soft-drink maker Cott Corp. (BCB-TSE), Rogers Communications Inc. (RCI.B-TSE), forest-products concern Repap Enterprises Inc. (RPP-TSE), and condominium developer Tridel Enterprises

(TDZ-TSE). Hindsight is twenty-twenty, but long-term investors would have been better off salvaging a few bucks from these stocks and buying something else.

> Another time to sell at least part of your stock is when a single stock becomes a big chunk of your overall savings. This can happen if you're lucky enough to own a great-performing stock for many years. There's no need to panic if you find that a single stock accounts for 5% or 10% of your savings, but once it starts getting up to 25% or more, you should probably take some action. If you're still saving, you might be able to reduce the stock's weighting in your portfolio by buying other stocks. If not, then you should consider selling a portion of your winning stock. It might seem counterintuitive to sell part of your best-performing stock, but remember that diversification is of upmost importance. If for some reason that lucky stock should crash and burn you won't feel too good about it. So if you own 200 shares of a stock that's 25% or more of your savings, it's a good idea to sell 50 or 100 shares and buy something else with the money (or go to Spain).

HURRY UP AND WAIT

If you own a stock that never seems to go up even after several years, you might be tempted to sell it. This is a very tough call, for some stocks that sit still for many years suddenly explode in value over one or two years. Others just putter along and go nowhere. Lean towards hanging on to a stock that stubbornly refuses to go up, especially if it's paying you a reasonable dividend. A stock that seems to edge lower year after year and doesn't pay a dividend is a better candidate for selling, unless it's merely tracking a broad stock-market decline.

Allow for more volatility for any stocks you might buy in emerging markets such as China, Southeast Asia, and South America.

Index Stocks

MUTUAL FUNDS WITHOUT THE FEES

You may have already heard about TIPS (R). TIPS 35 (TIP-TSE) and TIPS 100 (HIP-TSE) are TSE-traded securities that mimic the performance of the Toronto 35 Index (R) and the TSE 100 Index (R), respectively.

TIPS stands for Toronto Index Participation Units. These handy instruments allow investors to own a small piece of all of the same stocks that make up the Toronto 35 and TSE 100 indexes, and in the same proportion, by purchasing a single Toronto Stock Exchange listed security.

An investment in TIPS 35 is an investment in 35 of Canada's biggest companies, including:

- the major banks
- telecommunications giant BCE Inc. (BCE-TSE)
- auto-parts maker Magna International Inc. (MG.A-TSE)
- pipeline operator TransCanada PipeLines Ltd. (TRP-TSE)
- information provider Thomson Corp. (TOC-TSE)

- retailer Canadian Tire Corp. (CTR.A-TSE)

- transportation concern Bombardier Inc. (BBD.B-TSE)

- rail-transport company National Railway Co. (CNR-TSE)

- nickel and copper miner Inco Ltd. (N-TSE)

- oil producer Petro-Canada (PCA-TSE)

- booze and entertainment giant Seagram Co. (VO-TSE)

And an investment in TIPS 100 is an investment in 100 of Canada's biggest companies, including the companies that make up the Toronto 35 Index and TIPS 35, plus such names as:

- oil producer Alberta Energy Co. (AEC-TSE)

- retailer Hudson's Bay Co. (HBC-TSE)

- funeral home operator Loewen Group Inc. (LWN-TSE)

- supermarket concern Loblaw Cos. (L-TSE)

- health services company MDS Inc. (MHG.B-TSE)

- networking company Newbridge Networks Corp. (NNC-TSE)

- fertilizer maker Potash Corp. (POT-TSE)

- conglomerate Power Corp. of Canada (POW-TSE).

- airline Air Canada Inc. (AC-TSE)

- telecommunications company Teleglobe Inc. (TGO-TSE)

- brewer Molson Cos. (MOL.A-TSE)

All of the stocks that are included in the Toronto 35 and the TSE 100 (and thus TIPS 35 and TIPS 100) are also included in the TSE 300, an even broader index. There is no TIPS security for the TSE 300. See the TSE 300 Appendix at the end of this book for a complete list of the TSE 300 stocks, including those that are included in the Toronto 35 and the TSE 100 indexes (and thus TIPS 35 and TIPS 100).

TIPS 35 and TIPS 100 trade just like a stock. They're listed in the stock tables in the newspapers. You can buy them for inside or outside the RRSP for a one-time commission through a discount broker, and—presto—you have a highly diversified investment in the Canadian stock market, just like a mutual fund.

Unlike a typical mutual fund, however, the management expense ratio of the TIPS securities is hilariously low—0.05% or thereabouts per year in recent years. You've already been beaten over the head with the fact that the average Canadian mutual fund charged more than 2% per year in fees in 1997, though some MERs are closer to 1%. Even Canadian index funds have annual MERs in the 1% to 2% range.

With index stocks, you also receive the dividends paid by the companies in the index. These dividends paid by the companies included in TIPS 35 and TIPS 100 are collected and paid to all TIPS holders quarterly. As with any stock, if you're holding a TIPS stock inside your RRSP, the dividends won't be taxed. If held outside the RRSP, the dividends are subject to the same preferential tax treatment as any Canadian-company dividend.

Neither TIPS 35 nor TIPS 100 yet offer an automatic dividend reinvestment plan (DRIP) option (where dividends automatically go towards buying more of the same stock), but the TSE has been seeking to make one or both TIPS securities DRIP-eligible. Most investors would find a TIPS DRIP a convenient option when and if the service is offered. Check with your discount broker or the TSE periodically to see if the TIPS DRIP option is available.

Because companies pay dividends at various times and TIPS pays them only quarterly, there's a lag between the time some companies pay the dividends and when TIPS investors receive them. This means money owed to you can sit for a number of weeks before it's paid. It's a small price to pay for the simplicity and cost-effective TIPS method of investing. The annual dividend yields on the TIPS stocks at the moment are low—below 2%.

TIPS also differ from most mutual funds because capital-gains distributions on the TIPS securities are rare. Though TIPS 35 made a minor capital-gains distribution for 1997, a TSE official said this is expected to be a rare occurrence. This means you aren't likely to be doing Revenue Canada any favours even if you're holding TIPS outside your RRSP. As with any stock, of course, selling TIPS for a gain or loss outside an RRSP triggers the standard capital-gains tax rules.

The TSE plans to launch a TIPS-like investment for the new S&P/TSE 60 index, which contains many of the same stocks found in the Toronto 35 and the TSE 100.

> The Toronto Stock Exchange says its TIPS 35 was "the first-ever exchange-listed equity index product of its kind," when launched in 1990. For this invention the TSE can take a bow. Similar index-linked stocks are sprouting up all over the place. There are also index-linked stocks that track the Dow Jones Industrial Average (SM), the S&P 500 (R) index, the S&P MidCap 400 Index (R), and stock indexes that cover 17 different countries.

HOW INDEX STOCKS WORK

How do index stocks work? The short answer is that they represent ownership of a trust that buys the stocks that make up the index being imitated. But there's a fairly complex process behind the simplicity of investing in index stocks.

To understand how index stocks work, you must first understand how an index works. The Toronto 35, TSE 100, and TSE 300 operate in a similar fashion. The main determinant of whether a stock gets included in one of these indexes is its total market value, or capitalization. This is figured out by multiplying the company's stock price by the number of shares the company has outstanding, except for big blocks of shares that aren't usually up for sale. (For example, billionaire Ken Thomson owns a major portion of the shares of Thomson Corp. and doesn't trade them.) Then there are other considerations, such as whether a stock is actively traded, that determine if it's included in the indexes.

The stocks each have a different weighting in the indexes. This means some stocks, like BCE Inc. (BCE-TSE), for example, will have a much heavier weighting in the indexes because BCE is an exceptionally large company with a huge total market value compared with the rest of Canada's companies. BCE had a weighting of 5.70% on the TSE 300 at the end of 1997. Agnico-Eagle Mines Ltd. (AGE-TSE), a much smaller company, had a weighting of only 0.07% on the TSE 300 at the end of 1997. Generally speaking, the higher a stock climbs relative to all the other stocks in the index, the higher its weighting in the index will become.

Index stocks like TIPS are considered "passive" investments because you're just buying a basket of stocks without regard to the companies' merits, business plans, managements, or financial results, and you're holding the stocks for an indefinite period of time. But index stocks aren't entirely passive.

The indexes are reviewed periodically by the TSE. Because of changes in a company's market value and other factors, sometimes stocks get kicked out of the indexes and others take their place. Generally speaking, this means non-index stocks that are rising relatively quickly are likely to displace stocks in the index that aren't performing as well. Or, if a company in the index gets taken over, the company's stock will be replaced with another one. If you own TIPS or any of the other index stocks, those changes are all done for you.

TIPS AND THE TSE 300

The Toronto 35 Index and the TSE 100 Index, and thus TIPS 35 and TIPS 100, are strongly correlated with the performance of the TSE 300, the benchmark this book has been using to measure the performance of Canada's equity mutual funds.

The following chart shows the average annual compound rates of return for the three indexes, including dividends, to Dec. 31, 1997.

	1 Yr	3 Yr	5 Yr	10 Yr
TSE 300	14.98%	19.12%	17.46%	10.99%
Toronto 35	16.38%	20.18%	17.89%	11.32%
TSE 100	15.00%	19.19%	17.42%	11.12%

(Source: Toronto Stock Exchange)

TIPS 35 and TIPS 100, though they're based on the Toronto 35 Index and the TSE 100 Index, respectively, provide returns that are actually a shade behind the indexes' returns. This is mainly due to the dividend-payment lag noted above; some of your dividends are delayed before being paid out.

This chart shows the annual compound rates of return provided by TIPS 35, as compared to the Toronto 35 Index, for the periods ended April 30, 1998:

	TIPS 35	Toronto 35 Index
1 Year	31.54%	31.66%
3 Years	24.99%	25.17%
5 Years	18.78%	19.08%

(Source: The Toronto Stock Exchange)

The chart shows a typical variance between the TIPS securities and the corresponding index. The lag factor is minor—only 0.30 percentage points over five years in this case. That's far better than the one or two percentage points by which most mutual funds—even index funds—lag the market averages over long periods.

Note in the first chart that the returns of the three indexes tend to converge over long periods of time. The Toronto 35 and TSE 100 indexes, however, don't always move in lock-step with the TSE 300. Although each of the three indexes are influenced largely by the same heavily weighted stocks of Canada's biggest companies, the TSE 300 index contains many stocks not included in the other two. Still, the divergence factor between the Toronto 35 or the TSE 100 and the TSE 300 in recent years has clearly been much smaller than the 2% (or thereabouts) per year by which most Canadian equity mutual funds and most Canadian index mutual funds have trailed the TSE 300. The divergence seems to work in favour of the Toronto 35 or the TSE 100 rather than the TSE 300 index anyway, as the first chart above shows.

To find out all about TIPS and the TSE indexes, call the TSE at 1-888-TSE-8392 (or, in Toronto, at 416-947-4700) and ask for a prospectus for TIPS, or e-mail them at info@tse.com or check out the website at www.tse.com.

U.S. INDEX STOCKS

In the United States, three index stocks give investors a one-stop way to buy the biggest U.S. companies. These companies together make up the vast majority of the country's stock market value, though they total less than a thousand of the many thousands of U.S. companies traded on stock exchanges.

• DIAMONDS (SM) (DIA-AMEX) is an index stock that tracks the Dow Jones Industrial Average.

• Standard & Poor's Depositary Receipts (R) (SPY-AMEX), also known as SPDRs or "Spiders," is an index stock that tracks the S&P 500 index.

• Standard & Poor's MidCap 400 Depositary Receipts (TM) (MDY-AMEX), or MidCap SPDRs, track the S&P MidCap 400 Index.

These U.S. index-linked stocks are all traded on the American Stock Exchange (AMEX). They're eligible for your RRSP only to the extent that foreign securities are allowed.

To find out all about these U.S. index stocks, call 1-800-THE-AMEX (1-800-843-2639) and ask for prospectuses (no charge). At the time of this writing, the AMEX and the Nasdaq Stock Market were planning to merge, but hopefully the phone number hasn't changed. The prospectuses for the Spiders and Diamonds securities contain lists of all the stocks that make up the indexes.

The annual operating expenses on the U.S. index-linked stocks are amusingly low. For Diamonds it's about 0.18%; for S&P 500 SPDRs also about 0.18%; and about 0.30% for the MidCap SPDRs, according to their prospectuses.

The AMEX in late 1998 also launched nine index stocks for sub-indexes of the S&P 500, including consumer services, consumer staples, financial and technology.

The Dow Jones Industrial Average is probably the most widely recognized stock index in the world, even though it contains only 30 stocks. The S&P 500 is a much broader index, comprised of the biggest companies in the United States and a smattering of foreign companies. Most U.S. mutual fund managers compare their fund returns with the S&P 500.

The stocks that make up the DJIA are chosen by the editors of *The Wall Street Journal*. The DJIA is different from the TSE indexes or the S&P indexes in a few ways. Whether a stock is included in the TSE or S&P indexes is largely based on the market value of the company. The DJIA, on the other hand, is made up of stocks that the *Journal* editors feel represent a good cross-section of the U.S. economy, including criteria such as the company's market value.

DJIA Industrial Average as of spring 1998. All NYSE listed.

Alcoa (AA) — aluminum
AlliedSignal Inc. (ALD) — aerospace and automotive products
American Express Co. (AXP) — financial services
AT&T Corp. (T) — telecommunications
Boeing Co. (BA) — jets
Caterpillar Inc. (CAT) — farm and construction machinery
Chevron Corp. (CHV) — oil
Coca-Cola Co. (KO) — beverages
Walt Disney Co. (DIS) — theme parks, movies, entertainment
E.I. du Pont de Nemours & Co. (DD) — chemicals and plastics
Eastman Kodak Co. (EK) — film and photography
Exxon Corp. (XON) — oil
General Electric Co. (GE) — appliances, industrial products, aero-space, financial services; owns NBC television network
General Motors Corp. (GM) — cars and trucks
Goodyear Tire & Rubber Co. (GT) — tires
Hewlett-Packard Co. (HP) — computers
International Business Machines Corp. (IBM) — computers
Johnson & Johnson (JNJ) — health care products (Tylenol, Band-Aid etc.)
McDonald's Corp. (MCD) — fast food
Merck & Co. (MRK) — drugs
Minnesota Mining and Manufacturing Co. (MMM) — consumer products (more commonly known as 3M)

J.P. Morgan & Co. (JPM) — financial services

Philip Morris Cos. (MO) — cigarettes, food, beer (Marlboro, Kraft, Miller)

Procter & Gamble Co. (PG) — consumer and food products (Ivory soap, Cover Girl, Max Factor, Pampers, Crest, Cheer, Tide, Folger's, Pringles, etc.)

Sears, Roebuck and Co. (S) — department stores

Travelers Group Inc. (TRV) — financial services

Union Carbide Corp. (UK) — chemicals and plastics

United Technologies Corp. (UTX) — aerospace, building, automotive products.

Wal-Mart Stores Inc. (WMT) — department stores

The S&P 500 usually includes all of the DJIA stocks plus many more. Here are just a few of the bigger or better-known S&P 500 companies. A complete list is found in the Spiders prospectus or at www.standardand poors.com.

Abbott Laboratories (ABT-NYSE) — drugs

Allstate Corp. (ALL-NYSE) — insurance

Amoco Corp. (AN-NYSE) — oil

Anheuser-Busch Cos. (BUD-NYSE) — beer

Archer-Daniels-Midland Co. (ADM-NYSE) — agricultural commodities

BankAmerica Corp. (BAC) — banking

Bell Atlantic Corp. (BEL-NYSE) — telecommunications

BellSouth Corp. (BLS-NYSE) — telecommunications

Bristol-Myers Squibb Co. (BMY-NYSE) — drugs and health products

Chase Manhattan Corp. (CMB-NYSE) — banking

Chrysler Corp. (C-NYSE) — cars and trucks

Cisco Systems Inc. (CSCO-NASDAQ) — communications networks

Citicorp (CCI) — banking (planning merger with Travelers (TRV-NYSE))

Columbia/HCA Healthcare Corp. (COL-NYSE) — healthcare

Compaq Computer Corp. (CPQ-NYSE) — computers

Colgate-Palmolive Co. (CL-NYSE) — consumer products (Colgate, Mennen, Irish Spring, Palmolive, Ajax, Science Diet, etc.)

Crown Cork & Seal Co. (CCK-NYSE) — packaging

Deere & Co. (DE-NYSE) — farm and other machinery

Dell Computer Corp. (DELL-NASDAQ) — computers

Delta Air Lines Inc. (DAL-NYSE) — airline

Digital Equipment Corp. (DEC-NYSE) — computers

Dow Chemical Co. (DOW-NYSE) — chemicals

Dow Jones & Co. (DJ-NYSE) — information, newspaper publishing
(*The Wall Street Journal*, Dow Jones news and indexes)

Ford Motor Co. (F-NYSE) — cars and trucks

Fruit of the Loom Inc. (FTL-NYSE) — clothes

Gannett Co. (GCI-NYSE) — newspaper publishing

The Gap Inc. (GPS-NYSE) — clothing stores

General Mills Inc. (GIS-NYSE) — food (Cheerios, Wheaties, Betty
Crocker, Yoplait, etc.)

Gillette Co. (G-NYSE) — shaving supplies, batteries (Gillette, Braun,
Oral B, Duracell, etc.)

GTE Corp. (GTE-NYSE) — telecommunications

H.J. Heinz Co. (HNZ-NYSE) — ketchup and food

Hershey Foods Corp. (HSY-NYSE) — chocolate and food

Home Depot Inc. (HD-NYSE) — hardware stores

Intel Corp. (INTC-NASDAQ) — computer microprocessors

(Eli) Lilly & Co. (LLY-NYSE) — drugs

K Mart Corp. (KM-NYSE) — retailing

Kellogg Co. (K-NYSE) — food (Corn Flakes, Rice Krispies, Fruit
Loops, Eggo, Pop Tarts, etc.)

Lucent Technologies Inc. (LU-NYSE) — telecommunications equipment

Lockheed Martin Corp. (LMT-NYSE) — aerospace, defence

Mattel Inc. (MAT-NYSE) — toys and games

Merrill Lynch & Co. (MER-NYSE) — financial services

Microsoft Corp. (MSFT-NASDAQ) — computer software

Micron Technology Inc. (MU-NYSE) — semiconductors

Motorola Inc. (MOT-NYSE) — communications equipment

Nike Inc. (NKE-NYSE) — running shoes and sportswear

Oracle Systems Corp. (ORCL-NASDAQ) — computer software

J.C. Penney Co. (JCP-NYSE) — retailing

PepsiCo Inc. (PEP-NYSE) — soft drinks, snacks and fast food (Pepsi,
Mountain Dew, Frito-Lay, Pizza Hut, Taco Bell, KFC, etc.)

Pfizer Inc. (PFE-NYSE) — drugs and health products

Quaker Oats Co. (OAT-NYSE) — food and beverages (Quaker Oats,
Life cereal, Rice-A-Roni, Gatorade)

Reebok International Ltd. (RBK-NYSE) — shoes, clothes (Reebok,
Rockport, etc.)

Royal Dutch Petroleum Co. (RD-NYSE) — oil

Rubbermaid Inc. (RBD-NYSE) — household products

Sara Lee Corp. (SLE-NYSE) — food, clothes (Sara Lee, Jimmy Dean, Hanes, L'eggs, etc.)

Service Corp. Int'l (SRV-NYSE) — funeral homes, cemeteries

Sprint Corp. (FON-NYSE) — telecommunications

Sun Microsystems Inc. (SUNW-NASDAQ) — computers

Texas Instruments Inc. (TXN-NYSE) — computers, electronics, semiconductors, calculators, etc.

Time Warner Inc. (TWX-NYSE) — media (*Time, Life, Sports Illustrated*, HBO, Turner Broadcasting, CNN)

Toys R Us Co. (TOY-NYSE) — toy retailing

Unilever N.V. (UN-NYSE) — consumer products

Warner-Lambert Co. (WLA-NYSE) — drugs

Wells Fargo & Co. (WFC-NYSE) — bank

Wendy's International Inc. (WEN-NYSE) — Wendy's fast food (Tim Horton's)

WorldCom Inc. (WCOM-NASDAQ) — telecommunications

The S&P MidCap 400 index contains an entirely different set of U.S. stocks, ones with mid-size capitalizations or market values. Because the companies are smaller, you're less likely to have heard of them. Some of the more recognizable names include:

• America Online (AOL-NYSE)

• Cracker Barrel Old Country (CBRL-NASDAQ)

• Harley Davidson Inc. (HDI-NYSE)

• Office Depot Inc. (ODP-NYSE)

• Quaker State Corp. (KSF-NYSE).

The S&P MidCap 400 prospectus contains a full list of the stocks in the 400 index.

U.S. MUTUAL FUNDS VS. THE INDEX

As we've seen, Canadian mutual funds that invest in U.S. stocks have on average produced results well below the S&P 500. It's the same case with U.S. mutual funds. There's plenty of evidence showing that indexing has been the superior investment strategy over long periods of time in the United States. For example, check out these average annual returns to Dec. 31, 1997, according to

Barron's, a U.S. business weekly, and Lipper Analytical Services, which tracks U.S. mutual fund performance.

	DJIA	S&P 500	U.S. Stock Funds
1997 Return	24.9%	33.4%	24.3%
3 Yrs	30.1%	31.2%	24.7%
5 Yrs	22.0%	20.3%	16.7%
10 Yrs	18.6%	18.1%	15.8%

And the percentages of U.S. stock funds that topped the DJIA for the one-year, three-year, five-year, and 10-year periods to Dec. 31 were, respectively, 54.9%, 13.5%, 3.3%, and 12.6%.

INTERNATIONAL INDEX STOCKS

With index-linked stocks, the world is at your fingertips as well. The AMEX also offers WEBS, or World Equity Benchmark Shares (SM), which are index-linked stocks for 17 different countries. The indexes that these investments track are the country indexes created by Morgan Stanley Capital International (SM). There are 17 such indexes, one for each country.

The MERs for WEBS are higher than TIPS and Spiders, and averaged 1.12% as of May 31, 1998. This is still well below the average Canadian international mutual fund MER of 2.4% (for 1997), and on par with the lowest MERs.

The following list shows the AMEX-traded index-linked stocks for the various countries, the stock symbol, a comment about what sectors feature strongly in each index-linked stock, and a few names of the stocks you're buying.

> Call the AMEX WEBS line (1-800-810-9327) for an information package to get the whole story. Ask for a "Canadian Offering Circular" as well, to get the scoop on tax consequences and other issues for Canadians.

- **Australia**: (EWA-AMEX) banking, energy, metals, building materials, broadcasting & publishing, beverages & tobacco, real estate, etc. Stocks include Broken Hill Proprietary Ltd., National Australia Bank Ltd., News Corp., and Coca-Cola Amatil Ltd.

- **Austria**: (EWO-AMEX) banking, energy, machinery & engineering, construction, etc. Stocks include Bank Austria AG and VA Technologie AG.

- **Belgium**: (EWK-AMEX) insurance, gas & electric utilities, banking, energy, etc. Stocks include Electrabel SA, Fortis AG, and Petrofina SA.

- **France**: (EWQ-AMEX) health care, merchandising, banking, electronics, energy, etc. Stocks include Alcatel Alsthom, Elf Acquitaine SA, L'Oreal, and PSA Peugeot Citroen.

- **Germany**: (EWG-AMEX) automobiles, gas & electric utilities, telecommunications, banking, electronics, insurance, etc. Stocks include Daimler-Benz AG, Volkswagen AG, Deutsche Bank AG, BASF AG, Bayer AG, Siemens AG, Allianz AG, and Deutsche Telekom AG.

- **Hong Kong**: (EWH-AMEX) real estate, banking, telecommunications, utilities, etc. Stocks include Hutchison Whampoa Ltd., Sun Hung Kai Properties Ltd., and Hong Kong Telecommunications Ltd.

- **Italy**: (EWI-AMEX) banking, energy, insurance, telecommunications, etc. Stocks include Fiat SPA, ENI SPA, and Pirelli SPA.

- **Japan**: (EWJ-AMEX) banking, automobiles, electronics, machinery, chemicals, etc. Stocks include Matsushita Electric Industrial Co., Sony Corp., Honda Motor Co., Toyota Motor Corp., Hitachi Ltd., NEC Corp., Nikon Corp., Bridgestone Corp., Nippon Telegraph & Telephone Corp., and Fuji Photo Film Corp.

- **Malaysia**: (EWM-AMEX) banking, telecommunications, multi-industry, etc. Stocks include Telekom Malaysia BHD and Malayan Banking BHD.

- **Mexico**: (EWW-AMEX) beverages & tobacco, building materials, telecommunications. Stocks include Fomento Economico Mexicano SA, Kimberly-Clark de Mexico SA, and Telefonos de Mexico SA.

- **Netherlands**: (EWN-AMEX) energy, food & household products, broadcasting & publishing, chemicals, etc. Stocks include Philips Electronics NV, Akzo Nobel NV, Heineken NV, Royal Dutch/Shell, KLM, and Unilever NV.

- **Singapore**: (EWS-AMEX) banking, real estate, transportation, multi-industry, etc. Stocks include Singapore Airlines Ltd. and Singapore Telecommunications Ltd.

- **Spain**: (EWP-AMEX) banking, utilities, energy, telecommunications. Stocks include Banco Bilbao Vizcaya SA, Banco Santander SA, and Autopistas Concessionara Española SA.

- **Sweden**: (EWD-AMEX) electronics, health care, banking, forest products. Stocks include ABB, Ericsson, Volvo, and Astra AB.

- **Switzerland**: (EWL-AMEX) health care, banking, insurance, building materials, etc. Stocks include Novartis AG, Roche Holding AG, Nestle SA, Credit Suisse Group, Swiss Bank, and Union Bank of Switzerland.

- **United Kingdom**: (EWU-AMEX) banking, health care, telecommunications, merchandising, food & household products, etc. Stocks include Guiness Plc, British Petroleum Co, Glaxo Wellcome Plc, British Telecommunications Plc, and Smithkline Beecham Plc.

More WEBS are being planned for the following countries, if they haven't already been launched: Argentina, Brazil, Greece, Indonesia, Korea, Philippines, Portugal, South Africa, Thailand, Taiwan, and Turkey. Once these WEBS start trading, then even the emerging markets portion of your portfolio can be fulfilled with WEBS.

TAXATION AND FOREIGN INDEX STOCKS

Canadian investors must report all domestic and foreign income on their Canadian tax returns. Whether the foreign income is a dividend or otherwise, it is treated as regular income for Canadian tax purposes.

Just like any foreign stock, Spiders and WEBS pay dividends. They also make distributions of income and sometimes modest amounts of capital gains arising from transactions made within the Spiders or WEBS trusts. In the case of Spiders, dividends are paid quarterly (at the end of April, July, October, and January). WEBS make distributions in August and December.

> Any payout of dividends, income, or capital gains by Spiders and WEBS securities is made in U.S. dollars, is subject to U.S. withholding tax, and is treated as income for Canadian tax purposes. The standard withholding tax rate is 15%. Generally you can recoup such taxes withheld by claiming a foreign income tax credit on your tax return. (If the WEBS is held in your RRSP there is no such tax credit.)
>
>

In the case of WEBS, the country represented may withhold tax on distributions even before tax is withheld by the United States, and the country's withholding tax isn't eligible for a foreign income tax credit on a Canadian tax return. While this is a disappointing situation for Canadians, it shouldn't be a deterrent to buying WEBS either inside or outside the RRSP. For the most part, the dividend yields (which represent most of the distributions) on WEBS are usually small, and any withholding tax that can't be recouped is likely to be a small amount of money every year. International indexing is done for capital appreciation and diversification rather than regular income. Your outside-the-RRSP income-generating stock investments such as preferred shares and good dividend-paying stocks should be done with Canadian stocks, which makes tax treatment most favourable.

> If held outside the RRSP, you are responsible for including all Spiders and WEBS payouts (including taxes withheld) calculated in Canadian dollars in your annual tax return. These calculations should be done for you on your T5 mailed by your discount broker at year-end. You can usually receive a tax credit for the U.S. tax withheld by entering the tax paid to a foreign country in the federal foreign tax credit part of Schedule 1 of the Canadian tax return.

OTHER INTERNATIONAL INDEXING OPTIONS

Besides WEBS, there are some no-load fee-efficient ways to index internationally with Canadian mutual funds, and the choices are growing. For example, TD Green Line in late 1997 launched two funds that track foreign stock markets and are 100% RRSP eligible. The Green Line U.S. RSP Index Fund tracks the S&P 500 Index and has a maximum MER of 0.80%, a low figure but still substantially higher than the Spiders S&P 500 operating cost of 0.18%.

Green Line also launched the International RSP Index fund, which tracks the Morgan Stanley Capital International Europe, Australasia, Far East Index. According to the fund's prospectus, the proposed weighting will be about 34% in Japan, 20% in the United Kingdom, 12% in Germany, 8% in France, and smaller weightings in Hong Kong, Switzerland, Australia, The Netherlands, Sweden, Italy, and Spain. This fund's maximum MER is 1.25%.

Sporting an even lower MER is the CIBC International Index RRSP fund, with an MER of 0.90%. CIBC also offers an RRSP U.S. Index fund with a 0.90% MER. The First Canadian (Bank of Montreal) RRSP U.S. Equity Index fund MER is 1.22%.

How is it possible to index foreign countries with fully RRSP-eligible funds? It's made possible by the funds' use of futures contracts, a type of securities derivative that tracks foreign stock indexes while the funds still hold mostly Canadian money-market instruments that are RRSP eligible. Canada's tax rules stipulate that any income from such derivative investments must be taxed as income, rather than capital gains. The Green Line prospectus states that the U.S. and International index funds are intended for tax-sheltered plans such as RRSPs.

A few other low-MER international index funds have popped up. The Canada Trust International Equity Index fund has an MER of just 0.53%. And Altamira and Royal Bank in late 1998 launched Canadian, U.S. and International RRSP index funds with 0.5% MERs. These funds can make good sense for your RRSP, without using up foreign content.

INDEX-LINKED GICs

In the last few years a whole bunch of RRSP-eligible stock-index-linked GIC products have been made available to Canadian investors. View these products with skepticism, because most of them clip your potential returns in exchange for guaranteeing your principal—hardly an attractive trade-off.

> Getting your principal back if the stock index declines is no great shakes. Remember that any stock-market investor should be planning for the long haul, not just three or five years. You could get your index-linked GIC principal back only to watch the index finally surge higher. Index-linked GICs, however, can make sense for older folks who want stock-market exposure but can't afford to lose any principal.

Some index-linked GICs are tied to a variety of the world's major stock indexes. One such GIC pays interest linked to the performance of nine of the biggest industrial nations' stock indexes. There are hitches to these GICs as well. Some, for example, set maximum returns and don't pay the dividends that the stocks in the indexes pay. Also, the risk that the world's biggest stock markets will go down over long periods of time is minimal. If that does happen, we'll all be eating in soup kitchens anyway, guaranteed principal or no guaranteed principal.

Try to avoid locking in your stock investments. If you need the money, you won't be able to sell; and when the maturity dates come you'll be forced to sell. Younger people should steer clear of index-linked GICs. You don't want your stock investments to have a maturity date. Older investors might find them more appropriate.

THOUGHTS ON INDEXING

And now a few words on index-linked stocks. Indexing is an investment strategy that has been growing in popularity for many years. Because mutual funds haven't been able to keep up with the market averages, the logical, risk-averse investor should be happy with the market's average return or close to it.

But there are, of course, risks even when indexing. The most obvious one is that the world's stock markets will go down for many years and take all the indexers down with them, possibly even further than the mutual fund investors. In this case, the indexers will at least be able to point to mounds of statistical evidence in favour of their investment strategy, as they discuss their plight with everyone else on the bread lines.

> Another risk is "index mania." The popularity of indexing appears to be growing at an alarming rate. Some evidence suggests that at times there may be more money flowing into indexed investment strategies, at least in the United States, than into actively managed mutual funds. This trend has helped trigger a surge of demand for the stocks that make up the main stock indexes in North America. And this has clearly helped to push up valuations on the stocks in the S&P 500 and probably the TSE 300, compared with stocks not in those indexes. ⊙———▮

The TIPS securities, which took several years to catch on with the broad investing public, now rank among the most actively traded securities on a daily basis in Canada. There were a few billion dollars invested in TIPS in mid-1998, and probably several billion more invested in an indexed manner in the Canadian equity market.

As in the United States, indexed investment strategies have helped drive up the valuations on the stocks that make up the main stock indexes in Canada. Some folks on Bay Street shake their heads in disbelief at the stock-market valuations commanded by the big Canadian banks, BCE, the pipelines, utilities, and many of the others.

South of the border, on a price-to-earnings basis in spring 1998, the biggest of the big U.S. stocks, such as General Electric, Coca-Cola, Microsoft, and Gillette, tended to have the highest valuations among U.S. stocks. At that time, the P/E ratios of such stocks were in the 30s, 40s, or even higher. The S&P 500 overall P/E ratio was above 28, compared with a historic or traditional P/E ratio more like 18 or less.

> The P/E ratio, a company's stock price divided by its latest 12-months earnings per share, is the most widely used method of measuring a stock's valuation. Generally speaking, stocks of companies with above-average earnings growth have higher P/E ratios.

The long-term ramifications of a large percentage of investors adopting an indexed approach to stock-market investing are just plain freaky, and it's impossible to offer a reasonable prediction of what will happen if this type of situation comes to pass. Every time another person adopts an indexed approach to investing, the stocks that make up the index become a tiny bit more entrenched in that index, because they rise in value for reasons other than the performance of the company.

Will stocks in the indexes climb to the sky only to collapse when non-indexed investors bail out en masse and leave the indexers holding the bag? Who will be left to buy and sell the stocks in the main indexes if most people are passively holding the index? Will the biggest of the big stocks become so highly valued that they gobble up all the smaller companies with share-exchange transactions? It's a topic that makes for lively discussion over dinner, at least for the stock market geeks among us.

These questions, we hope, are more philosophical than practical. It seems fairly safe to predict that for many years to come there will be enough stock market "gamblers" out there to allow indexers their hands-off approach to investing. In mid-1998, the amount of money tracking the S&P 500 was measured in the hundreds of billions of dollars, while the overall U.S. stock market was valued in the several trillions of dollars.

If you decide on an indexed approach for all your investments, do yourself a favour. Don't index just one country; go with several. And don't devote your entire savings to one index fund, even if it is multinational. Staying diversified, remember, means having several different types of investments, and some index funds can fail to closely mimic their benchmarks. Use the 20% foreign content allowed in your RRSP. And remember that the Canadian stock market moves very much in tandem with the U.S. stock market (but never seems to keep up over the long term), so be sure to index some countries outside of North America. You'll be glad you did if North American stock markets turn sour.

To wrap up, nobody can guarantee that index-linked stocks will always outperform the average mutual fund they are matched against over the long term, but historical evidence and logic sure make it hard to argue otherwise.

CHAPTER NINE

Diversification

MINIMIZING RISK IN YOUR PORTFOLIO

Diversification is a word we've touched on a few times already, and now we're going to harp on it. Diversification is an absolute top priority for any investor, especially the do-it-yourselfer. It reduces risk. The more you diversify your investments, the less risk you take that one of them will singlehandedly drag your overall portfolio substantially lower.

WHAT IS DIVERSIFICATION?

Diversification means spreading out your money into different types of investments, such as stocks, bonds, and your house, or at least planning to spread out your investments as you save more. It means having money invested in many different companies in different industries. It means having your investments exposed to different countries and therefore different currencies. It means having bonds that mature at different times.

R epeat this word over and over: DIVERSIFY. Sing it out loud. Sit in a circle with your friends and hold hands while everyone chants: DIVERSIFY. Write the word DIVERSIFY backwards on your forehead and look in the mirror. Name your cat DIVERSIFY.

You should DIVERSIFY your investments, and practise DIVERSI-FICATION so that your investments are DIVERSIFIED.

The *Random House College Dictionary* defines "diversified" as "distributed among or producing several types: diversified investments." Even the dictionary knows about sound investing.

I'm constantly amazed by the number of people who claim to know about the importance of diversification, but don't practise it themselves.

A friend of mine has had a big chunk of his life savings on Bank of Montreal (BMO-TSE) for several years. Lucky for him, it's damn near made him rich. But can you imagine how he would feel today if that stock hadn't performed well, or if it had gone down over the last several years? He would be a miserable person indeed. Having most of your savings on one stock, even a good one, is not being diversified!

Another do-it-yourself investor I know (who works in the mutual fund industry, I might add) likes to play the U.S. technology stocks. His investments, however, aren't anywhere near as diversified as the U.S. technology scene, which is huge. At one point a big portion of his investments were on a few "search-engine" stocks, the companies that make software to roam the Internet. This is not diversification! The search-engine industry could be a flash in the pan, for all we know, and these stocks could come crashing down. To top it off, this person was borrowing money to buy his stocks—a technique known as buying "on margin." This guy's risk was through the roof.

I was once at an annual meeting for Echo Bay Mines Ltd. (ECO-TSE), a gold mining company. After the presentation, a woman approached the chief executive officer. She was clearly distressed about the company's long-falling stock price.

"My husband has a big part of our retirement savings on Echo Bay," she said indignantly. "What are you going to do about it?"

The CEO politely explained that he was doing everything in his power to make Echo Bay succeed and command a higher stock price. I wanted to give the woman a swat on the head with a rolled-up newspaper, but instead suggested that she shouldn't put all of her eggs in one basket.

Lack of diversification is what destroyed my grandmother's life savings. On the advice of a lawyer acting as her financial advisor, coupled with her own lack of knowledge about sound investing, about 20 years ago she put most of her money into a fund that invested in a few real-estate projects. After a few years of lousy real estate markets, the real-estate developers were unable to make the interest payments, and the fund investors to this day are trying to get back their initial investment. Many Toronto-area people, including a few celebrities, were caught in this fund. Hopefully they were better diversified than my grandmother.

Even sadder than these examples is the Bre-X Minerals story. The infamous gold-fraud fiasco claimed many, many victims; some had a large part of their net worth on the stock. According to news reports, at least two men killed themselves after meeting with financial ruin caused by the collapse of Bre-X.

DIVERSIFICATION WITH INDIVIDUAL STOCKS

If you choose an index-linked stock approach to investing, your portfolio will be highly diversified as long as you make sure to keep a meaningful proportion outside of North America.

The investor who chooses individual stocks instead of index stocks or in conjunction with index stocks, however, must be very careful to remain properly diversified while building a savings portfolio. The individual stock investor must also be aware that his or her returns will be different from the market averages.

> An individual stock investor can achieve adequate diversification with fewer stocks than you might think. Being diversified and minimizing risk doesn't mean you have to hold 186 different stocks and bonds in your portfolio.

"Fortunately for the average investor, it is not necessary to hold all 2,081 New York Stock Exchange listed stocks to benefit substantially from diversification," wrote Alan C. Shapiro in his textbook *Modern Corporate Finance* (Macmillan Publishing Co., New York, 1990 page 107). In fact, he wrote, "Most of the benefits of diversification can be achieved with as few as 10 different stocks."

Though you cannot eliminate risk, you can sharply reduce the chances that your returns will stray far from the stock market's average returns. If you own only one stock, say, of a thousand stocks listed on an exchange, your risk is a hundred percent compared with the overall movement of all the stocks on the exchange. Your stock could tumble to zero over a few years while the stock index marches merrily upwards. Or your stock could zoom ahead while the market average sputters along going nowhere.

If you own two stocks, your risk is reduced but it's still a highly volatile portfolio. Owning three, four, or five stocks is safer, but is still very risky. When you approach 20 stocks of companies in various industries, your portfolio becomes very diversified. Buying more stocks than that only slightly decreases your risk further, compared with the overall market average.

OTHER EGGS IN OTHER BASKETS

Academics also point out that international investing reduces risk. That means if you include some European, Asian, and/or South American stocks in your portfolio, your risk will be lower than if you only buy Canadian and/or North American stocks. So if you decide to invest without index stocks, you can build a diversified portfolio of big-company stocks by picking as few as 20 stocks from North America and around the world!

However, this doesn't mean 20 stocks that are all in the same industry! Nor does it mean 20 stocks of start-up companies hoping to bring a product to market one day, or mining companies or oil and gas companies that don't actually produce any metals or oil and gas. Nor does it mean 20 stocks that don't pay any dividends, or 20 stocks that all pay hefty dividends. It doesn't mean 20 stocks of very small companies.

The key to reducing risk in your stock portfolio is to own a good mix of several different stocks that have different characteristics. These characteristics include the company's industry, the countries it is based in and does business in, and the factors that affect the company's stock price (such as its dividend yield, the size of the company, and other factors). ⊙

This book contains a list of the 300 stocks in the TSE 300 as of early 1998, and some notes about their characteristics, to help you choose a diversified portfolio.

And most of the companies should have an established track record, which means they have been selling a product or service for several years—not that they're planning to bring a product to market one day. (All but a few companies named in this book pass this test.)

If you're investing only with individual stocks, you should have at least 20 different ones in order to achieve diversification and minimize risk. Another approach, however, is to invest with a mixture of individual stocks and index stocks. This requires fewer individual stocks while still allowing sound diversification. ⊙

Buying individual stocks doesn't require any special knowledge about the company you're investing in, and it offers the potential for returns above the market averages. Investors who do decide to buy individual stocks, however, should be aware that their investment returns could also lag the index returns. We'll discuss individual stock investing much more as we continue.

INTERNATIONAL EXPOSURE

You may have read that Canada's stock market represents a mere 3% of the world's stock-market capitalization, or the total value of all the stocks in the world. This would imply that a diversified portfolio would include some investments outside of Canada. True; but it doesn't mean you have to invest everywhere from Albania to Zimbabwe to be soundly diversified.

In fact, you can achieve a good deal of your diversification while staying at home in good old Canada! We have many large companies with broad international operations. Just because Canada's stock-market value is only 3% of the world doesn't mean you keep a mere 3% of your money here. The current RRSP rules restrict you in this regard anyway.

Take a look around—most of what you see is a terrifically high standard of living compared with 90% of the world's population. This is no fluke—we Canadians didn't just happen upon prosperity. We're highly educated, motivated, capable, and among the most creative people on the planet! Those traits aren't going to disappear tomorrow. And foreigners, many skilled and eager to work, will be lining up to get into Canada for many decades to come. (Now if we could only get all the homeless people some food and a place to live. Here's a proposal: Let's all stop paying fees to mutual fund companies and stockbrokers and give a generous chunk of that money to the people who really need it!)

For an example of stay-at-home diversification, take the big Canadian banks. Notwithstanding the above-mentioned riskiness of owning one Canadian bank stock for the bulk of an investment portfolio, all of Canada's banks are highly diversified companies. They lend money to a wide variety of businesses here and around the world. They all operate full-service and discount brokerage firms, which make money from securities underwriting, trading, and other services. Most banks own part of several foreign banks around the world. They all sell mutual funds. They own trust companies and insurance companies. By golly, the big Canadian bank stocks are almost like little mutual funds in themselves!

Or take BCE Inc. (BCE-TSE), one of Canada's biggest companies. BCE operates Bell Canada, which provides local and long-distance telephone service for most people in Quebec and Ontario, and other communications services such as the Internet and voice mail. Bell also owns a major stake in Northern Telecom Ltd. (NTL-TSE), which provides telecommunications equipment to companies literally around the planet. BCE has other international operations as well. We're talking solid diversification in a single stock.

How about Thomson Corp. (TOC-TSE)? This is a big company that owns newspapers, electronic information databases, and publishing interests in Canada, the United States, Europe, and elsewhere. And Potash Corp. (POT-TSE) sells fertilizer all over the globe. TrizecHahn Corp. (TZC-TSE) owns commercial real estate in Canada, the United States, Europe, and elsewhere. Seagram Co. (VO-TSE) sells its booze and entertainment all around the world. Bombardier Inc. (BBD.B) sells airplanes, jets, jet skis, and other products in many different countries, and Magna International Inc.'s (MG.A-TSE) auto parts are bought by auto makers in North America, Europe, and elsewhere. Newbridge Networks Corp. (NNC-TSE), Teleglobe Inc. (TGO-TSE), and Telesystem International Wireless Inc. (TIW-TSE) are a few of Canada's companies selling telecommunications products and services all over the map. And the Canadian pipeline companies and several power utilities are making inroads in developing countries.

> Hey, you can even invest where Americans aren't supposed to tread: Cuba. Sherritt International Corp. (S-TSE) has its foot into Cuban mining, tourism, energy, power, and telecommunications, with plans to do much more. ◉————

These are just a few of the internationally diversified investments you can make with stocks in the TSE 300. Check the TSE 300 list included in this book for more ideas about international diversification with Canadian stocks (see Appendix).

Alas, even buying Canadian stocks with international exposure doesn't reduce your risk that the Canadian stock market will go down, because all stocks in one particular stock market tend to move in the same direction over long periods of time. That's why when seeking international diversification with an individual stock approach, it's important to invest in some stocks abroad. The easiest way to do this is with a few WEBS or a low-MER international fund, but you can also buy individual stocks of companies based abroad. Many are listed on the New York Stock Exchange, and we'll discuss them in Chapter 11.

DIVERSIFIED PORTFOLIO STRATEGIES

Whether you're buying index stocks, individual stocks, or a combination of both, as a long-term investor you can take comfort in the fact you're paying very low fees to invest, which is a big advantage over mutual funds.

The cost of buying stocks, however, should be taken into account when choosing an approach. It's not very economical, for example, for an investor with under $5,000 to buy 20 different stocks, since it would cost at least $500 in commissions to buy them. This investor is probably better off with an index stock or two, possibly branching out into small amounts of other stocks later. Younger investors can tolerate higher risk, or lower diversification, but should be ever-mindful of increasing diversification as they go.

Below are some different approaches for building a diversified portfolio of big-company stocks. The approaches apply to your overall stock portfolio, and don't take into account what's inside and what's outside your RRSP. That's your job to figure out.

THE ALL-INDEX STOCKS APPROACH

The all-index stocks investor buys only TIPS 35 and/or TIPS 100 for Canadian content, Spiders and/or Diamonds for U.S. stock investing, and WEBS and/or a low-MER international index mutual fund for international diversification.

This investor is content with the market averages of the chosen countries, because low-fee indexing tends to outperform most mutual funds. The simplicity of index investing is another plus. This investor may also consider buying a small-cap equity fund or two for added diversification (and, possibly, higher returns).

THE INDEX STOCKS AND A LUCKY STOCK APPROACH

This investor has 90% or more of her stock investments in index stocks, and an individual stock just to keep things interesting and add some "spin" to her returns.

She is like the all-index stock investor, but enjoys following a single stock, which might provide her with above-average returns.

THE INDEX STOCKS AND SOME OTHER STOCKS APPROACH

This investor will have anywhere from 50% to 90% of the total value of her stock investments on a few index stocks, and the remainder on individual company stocks with different character-istics. With 65%-90% on index stocks she should have at least three other stocks, but five or more would be even better. With 50%-65% on index stocks she should have at least five other stocks, but a few more would be even better. Her other stocks should have some international diversification and she should seek out a no-load small-cap fund or two to round out her portfolio.

This investor wants to take a moderate amount of added risk in return for a shot at above-average returns, and accepts that her returns will moderately or substantially outperform or underper-form the market averages.

THE INDEX STOCKS BUT MOSTLY OTHER STOCKS APPROACH

This investor has a few index stocks making up as much as 50% of his equity investments, but most of his stock investments are in individual stocks. With 35% to 50% of his stock investments indexed, he should have at least eight other stocks. With 15% to 35% indexed he should have at least 12 other stocks. The individ-ual stocks should be highly diversified by characteristics and have a healthy dose of international flavour. He should seek to include a small-cap fund or two as well.

This investor accepts that his stock returns are only slightly tied to the market averages, and he accepts that his returns will mod-erately or substantially outperform or underperform the market averages.

The Tilted Index Approach

This approach applies to the Canadian stock portion of a portfolio. It involves buying all of the non-cyclical stocks (about 20) in the Toronto 35 index for the Canadian equity component of a diversified portfolio. Based on long-term historical trends in the Canadian market, this approach has a good shot at outperforming the TSE 300 over the long term. You'll still need a healthy dose of WEBS or international stock action and a small-cap fund or two. See the TSE 300 chapter for a full explanation of this approach.

The All-Stock Approach

For the true do-it-yourselfer. Also for ethically minded do-it-yourself investors. This type doesn't even bother with index stocks. He has a bare minimum of 20 stocks with many different characteristics, including several from other countries besides Canada and the United States. More stocks would be even better. He's still likely to hold a small-cap fund or two. He usually likes to put a bit more time into picking his stocks, which he plans to hold for the long term. He probably subscribes to a newspaper with a good business section and he might occasionally do some research through his discount broker, on the Internet, in the library, or elsewhere. These tools help him narrow down his investments to stocks he feels have solid long-term potential and fit with his ethical standards. His research will also help him decide if it's ever time to sell a stock. He might be a member of an investment club.

This investor realizes that his returns aren't tied to the market averages. This doesn't bother him because he knows that a properly diversified portfolio of long-term investments is a sound investment strategy.

The above approaches aren't carved in stone, and your portfolio will constantly be shifting with movements in the markets and new investments that you make. As time goes by you might find that you're no longer in line with your approach. Don't sweat it. For example, if you buy mainly index stocks but have a few others as well, you may get lucky with your other stocks and find that their value grows to even more than your index stocks (wouldn't that be nice?). Consider selling to bring the proportion back in line. Or plan for future investments to bring you back in accord with your plan. Use common sense to keep your portfolio diversified and on track.

The TSE 300

YOUR GUIDE TO A DIVERSIFIED CANADIAN STOCK PORTFOLIO

In this chapter we discuss individual stock picking and the TSE 300. A complete list of the TSE 300 stocks is in the Appendix at the end of this book.

WHY BUY INDIVIDUAL STOCKS?

You might be thinking, "Why would I buy any individual stocks if the index always beats most mutual funds and I can buy index stocks?" It's a good question. You don't have to buy individual stocks. But here are a few reasons why you might decide to buy at least a few:

1. Doing so offers the potential for higher (but also lower) returns than the index.

2. It can reduce your exposure to "cyclical" stocks, which are included in TIPS 35 and TIPS 100 and have long underperformed the TSE indexes.

3. It can increase the dividend yield of your portfolio, if you buy stocks that pay good dividends.

4. There are 200 stocks in the TSE 300 that aren't part of TIPS 35 and TIPS 100.

5. It's fun and educational to own shares of a company.

YOUR PICKS ARE AS GOOD AS ANY PRO'S

"But by golly, I can't buy my own stocks. I don't know anything about the stock market!"

Many of you have probably uttered a comment like that before. Let's do a quick examination of how the stock market works, and then you can decide how much you have to know about it before choosing suitable big-company stocks yourself.

A company's stock makes it into a stock index such as the TSE 300 because many people own it and the company has a large stock-market value. If you buy a stock that's part of a major stock index, you are merely joining a list of thousands of investors who already own the stock for one reason or another.

Some investors think they or their brokers have to do an in-depth study on a company and its stock before it can be purchased. Occasionally this does help some investors make above-average stock picks, but for investing in big-company stocks like the ones in the TSE 300 it isn't necessary.

It's not as if you have to pass a test on the company's business prospects and financial statistics to own the company's stock. The company's board of directors doesn't call a special meeting just because you bought 100 shares.

As long as you know a few main points about the company—such as which industry it's in, whether it's still in the index, and whether it pays a good dividend—you can make good decisions. Beyond that, you don't need a reason to buy a particular company's stock. You can do it for the same reason mountain climbers risk their lives climbing Mount Everest: because it's there.

An investor can learn all he wants about a particular company, memorize its income statement and balance sheet, eat dinner three times a week with the CEO, and spend four hours a day on the company's shop floor, but it won't help one iota with the ultimate question: How much will somebody else pay me for my stock when I want to sell it? That's a question that nobody can answer.

Take, for example, Canadian Pacific Ltd. (CP-TSE), the big railway, hotel, oil, and transportation company. Imagine that a mutual fund manager who holds some CP shares in his fund is sitting in his office high atop one of Toronto's office towers. He pulls out CP's latest quarterly financial report and does some number crunching. "Hmm," he says, "it looks like CP's profit margins on its grain-transport lines are off this quarter, and they're calling for dry weather out west this summer. That means the farmers in Alberta might not be able to repeat last year's bumper wheat crops, which could leave CP's transport trains only half-full this fall." The fund manager figures he's already made $9 a share on CP and that the stock is likely to tumble, so he taps in an order on his computer to sell 100,000 CP shares at $48 each.

At the exact same time, two office towers over, a pension fund manager is eyeballing CP's latest quarterly report and its stock price. He's impressed by the increasing numbers of people staying in CP-owned hotels across Canada, and he read somewhere that 10% more Americans are planning a trip to Canada this year over last year for their vacations. "And that 12-months out price-to-earnings ratio of 11 plus the low debt-to-total capitalization and $65 break-up value look sweet," the pension fund manager mutters to himself. The pension fund manager thinks CP is going higher, so he puts in an order to buy 100,000 shares at $48. The trade goes through.

At the end of the day, the pension fund manager and the mutual fund manager meet for a beer and argue the entire time about who the best goalie in the NHL is. Neither has any clue they traded 100,000 shares of CP with each other that day.

The point here is that although the two fund managers both had good reasons for doing what they did, they can't both be right about the future of CP's stock price. This type of situation plays out every minute of every day the stock market is open for trading, all around the world.

Also, relying on "professional" advice about stock picking is usually no better than going with your own instincts. Professional advice can be slanted or as old as the hills. For example, there's a word that isn't in the vocabulary of most Bay Street financial analysts: "sell." There's little to be gained by an analyst for Akinson Backinson Securities Co. that utters this word—or worse, places it at the top of a thick report about Monstrous Industries Ltd. Akinson Backinson, you see, might be overlooked the next time Monstrous calls upon a bunch of securities firms to sell to investors shares or convertible debentures of Monstrous. Securities firms generate juicy fees from underwriting such issues for companies.

But my Broker Recommended...

This brings us to the "buy" recommendation, a daily pronouncement in the canyons of Bay Street. The "buy" recommendation ensures that nobody gets mad at anybody else (unless the stock plummets). The client of a stockbroker panting on the phone about how Monstrous is a "buy" should resist the urge to think he's the early bird catching the worm. Often, the broker's nine colleagues were already spreading the good word about Monstrous, as was the financial analyst who came up with the "buy."

Another thing you need to know about the stock market is that the "pros" are often nowhere in sight just before a stock goes on a big tear or is about to sink, so relying on them to get you in and out of the right stocks at the right time is usually folly. Remember my friend with his life savings on Bank of Montreal? His stockbroker called him up one day telling him to buy Newbridge Networks Corp. (NNC-TSE), because it had fallen from $92 to $42 in a matter of months and was "cheap." Three days later Newbridge warned of a poor quarter for earnings and the stock fell more than $10 in a matter of seconds.

And few, if any, among the learned financial community (and the business news media), were openly casting aspersions on Bre-X Minerals Ltd. before the scam fell apart like a house of cards. How many analysts were negative on Philip Services Corp. (PHV-TSE) before the recycler's stock sank like a stone in early 1998, when the company blamed massive writedowns on a long-simmering copper-trading scandal? Few financial types were pounding the

table warning about the impending demise of the following spectacular flameouts: Tee-Comm Electronics Inc., Hookup Communications Corp., Royal Trustco Inc., Anvil Range Mining Corp., and
Gandalf Technologies Inc.

To be sure, there were plenty of warnings made both by financial analysts and the financial press on some of Canada's laggardly
stocks. Software company Corel Corp. (COS-TSE) and its gutsy but
star-crossed challenge to Microsoft come to mind. So do the moun-
tains of debt piled up by television cable company Rogers Communications Inc. (RCI.B-TSE) and paper-maker Repap Enterprises Inc.
(RPP-TSE). And private-label soft drink company Cott Corp. (BCB-
TSE) and its strong sales but skimpy profits were well documented
in the newspapers before and during the stock's long decline.

Finally, a word about the dreaded "consensus earnings estimate," a mainstay of the professional investing world. This beast is
the mean earnings-per-share estimate of all financial analysts who
follow a particular company's stock. The consensus earnings estimate is published by a few corporate information providers and is
often circulated on the Internet. Every time a widely followed company is about to release its quarterly earnings, analysts, fund managers, shareholders, and other financial types gather 'round the
newswires to watch the numbers come out. The idea is that a company's earnings per share must top the "consensus estimate," or
investors will send the company's stock into a death spiral.

Not wanting to be the victim of any such stock selloff, companies all across the land have developed a skill for playing down
earnings expectations when talking to analysts ahead of quarter
end. This ensures that none of the analysts get too carried away
with their estimates. But of course the analysts often are hip to this
racket, which has led to the even more dreaded "whisper number."
This is the unpublished consensus estimate among analysts and
institutional investors who are in the loop and wise to the company's shenanigans. Companies then have to top the whisper number or have their stock face certain death. Problem is, you're never
quite sure what the whisper number is, or if there is one at all, and
these days all kinds of different whisper numbers are plastered all
over the Internet.

All of this leaves bewildered business journalists, such as yours
truly, unable to answer copy editors' questions from New York:

"It says here in your story that the company's earnings per share topped the analysts' consensus estimate, but the stock went down. Why?"

"I don't know," I say. "If I knew that, then I'd be writing the story from my island in the Caribbean while sipping expensive wines between chapters of my memoirs."

The above examples are all meant to show you that gamesmanship is never-ending in the stock market, and that getting the scoop from supposedly knowledgeable sources is hardly ever really getting the scoop.

GETTING TO KNOW THE TSE 300

So we'll now turn to the TSE 300. Whether you're building an all-stock portfolio or looking for a few stocks to round out your index-linked stocks, the TSE 300 list of companies will help you make good stock selections in a short period of time.

The Appendix contains a list of the TSE 300 as of March 1998. The list shows each stock's weighting in the index. (A stock's weighting is its ever-changing rank in the index, as measured roughly by market value; it reflects the stock's influence on the index.)

The list shows the stock symbol and which industry the company is in. There may be a brief comment about the company. "T35" indicates if it's a member of the Toronto 35 index and therefore TIPS 35. "T100" indicates the stock is in the TSE 100 index and therefore TIPS 100. "DIVIDEND" indicates that the company's stock has traditionally paid a good dividend.

The Toronto Stock Exchange Review is a monthly publication put out by the TSE, and is a great guide for Canadian stock investors. To get a copy you can write to TSE Publications, The Exchange Tower, 2 First Canadian Place, Toronto, ON, Canada M5X 1J2. Or phone them at 416-947-4681 (or fax them at 416-814-8811) to order one. *The Review* is $22.47 for a single copy or $199.02 for a subscription, but call first to make sure the price hasn't changed. You can also find *The Review* in the magazine rack of many bookstores, selling for about $13. You should get a copy of *The Review* once a year when you do the annual checkup on your investments. More hands-on investors might want to buy it more often or get a subscription.

The Review has tons of statistics in it. What's most useful about it is contained in the green pages at the back, where all the TSE 300, Toronto 35, and TSE 100 stocks are listed, showing weightings, industry groupings, and other stuff. Note that the TSE 300 stocks are listed twice—once by industry group and once by weighting. *The Review*'s blue pages contain information about each stock's trading activity, dividend payouts, dividend yield, number of shares outstanding, earnings per share, and price-to-earnings ratio.

If you're looking for a few good dividend-paying stocks to round out your TIPS stocks, then scan the TSE 300 list in the Appendix for stocks with DIVIDEND noted after them. To find the current dividend yield, check a newspaper or get a current copy of *The Review* and look in the blue pages. Remember that a 3 % dividend yield or higher on a common stock is a lot these days.

By adding a few dividend-paying stocks to your TIPS investments, you'll increase your portfolio's overall dividend yield; this is good for more cautious, income-seeking investors. If, for example, the TIPS stocks are yielding about 1.8 % per year, then an investor could buy a few stocks with dividend yields above 4 % to raise the overall dividend yield of the portfolio. Cash dividends paid inside the RRSP build up and can be used to make new investments. Dividends paid outside the RRSP are taxed at a lower rate than other income and can be used for making new investments or for spending money.

If you're an all-stock investor or a mostly-other-stocks investor (rather than TIPS) for your Canadian equity portfolio, then be sure to pick out a diversified selection of stocks from the TSE 300. The portfolio should be anchored with several big-weighting blue-chip stocks, should contain stocks in different industries, and should have some that pay dividends.

> As you familiarize yourself with the TSE 300, take note of the weightings of the various stocks and sectors. Allow your stock picks to be influenced by the weightings.

This is to say, for example, that since the biggest six Canadian bank stocks collectively account for more than 20 % of the weighting of the TSE 300, a non-TIPS Canadian stock portfolio should have a healthy dose of bank action. Similarly, note that BCE Inc. (BCE-TSE) and the other telephone companies make up a large combined percentage of the TSE 300, so holding BCE and/or a few other telephone stocks is a good idea. There's no need to mirror the TSE 300 weighting exactly, but the more your stock picks mirror the TSE 300 weightings, the more your returns will be tied to the TSE 300 returns.

> **B**e conscious of whether your individual stocks are already included in any TIPS shares you own. It's okay if they are; just recognize that you are "doubling down" to a certain extent on that particular stock. To double down on a big-weighting stock like BCE (6.99% of TSE 100 weighting March 1998) or the Canadian banks will significantly increase your overall exposure to that stock if you already own TIPS, as long as those stocks continue to have big weightings. To buy a smaller stock, say with a 0.3% weighting in the TSE 100, isn't really doubling down much, because the 0.3% wasn't much of your portfolio in the first place. (TSE 100 weightings are listed in *The Review.*)

THE CHECKUP

We'll touch on this now, and go over it in detail later. Every do-it-yourself investor must do a periodic checkup. There's a quick monthly checkup to see if you have cash to invest, and a more detailed annual checkup, when you examine your financial situation in detail. If the monthly checkup shows you have some extra cash to invest, then invest it!

The annual checkup is more detailed. This is when you grab a copy of the *TSE Review* at least once a year for a thorough examination of your financial situation. This is when you check to make sure your Canadian stocks are still in the TSE 300. If one of your stocks is no longer there, take it out behind the barn and shoot it! Sell it, no matter what price it's at. Never mind the capital gain or the capital loss; just dump that stock like a bag of garbage.

The strategy of selling any stocks that get the boot from the TSE 300 is by no means perfect. But what it does is roughly ensure that you're not holding a stock that can't keep up with the pack. When you get to the bottom 25 stocks or so in the TSE 300, you're usually talking about some pretty rinky-dink companies, or ones that aren't doing very well. You may decide to sell a stock long before it ever gets kicked out of the TSE 300. For example, you may decide to shoot any stock that gets below a 0.05% TSE 300 weighting. Or you might decide to own only stocks that are in the TSE 100, and sell any that fail to remain in that index.

CYCLICAL STOCKS

Long-term investors would probably do well to avoid "cyclical" stocks. Cyclical stocks tend to belong to natural-resource companies such as mining companies, forest-product companies, steel companies, oil and gas companies, and some real-estate companies. Cyclical stocks, as the name implies, tend to move with economic cycles rather than climbing steadily. They go up quickly when times are good for the company, and go down quickly when things look bad. All too often, the cyclical stock winds up right where it started several years before, which is no good to the long-term investor.

Many long-term shareholders of Canada's best-known resource companies have watched teary-eyed from the sidelines while their investments went nowhere during the 1990s bull market, and in some cases much longer. Shares of several of the big names in the Canadian resource sector—such as miners Noranda Inc. (NOR-TSE), Inco Ltd. (N-TSE), and Cominco Ltd. (CLT-TSE); forest-products concerns MacMillan Bloedel Ltd. (MB-TSE) and Domtar Inc. (DTC-TSE); steel producers Dofasco Inc. (DFS-TSE) and Stelco Inc. (STE.A); and several oil and gas stocks—have been long-term laggards.

> If it weren't for Canada's resource stocks, the TSE 300 index would have produced returns much closer to the astonishing returns posted by the U.S. stock indexes over the past few decades. Returns for the metals and minerals, gold and precious metals, paper and forest products, oil and gas, and real estate subgroups of the TSE 300 are well below those for other sectors and well below the TSE 300.

In fact, these days the resource stocks are being weeded out of the TSE indexes. For example, all seven of the stocks that got kicked out of the TSE 300 under the exchange's annual review in late 1997 are resource stocks: three gold miners, three oil and gas companies, and one fertilizer company. Of the seven replacement stocks, two were insurance companies; one was a building materials company; one was a high-tech manufacturing equipment company; one was a real estate company; and one was an oil-industry service company (not a pure resource stock). One company, a miner, was a pure resource company. Also, of the nine stocks that got the boot from the TSE 100 index in early 1998, six were resource stocks (four miners, an oil, and a forest). None of the nine replacement stocks were resource related.

Canada's resource stocks today have less influence on the main stock indexes. The stocks that make up the TSE's metals and minerals, gold and precious metals, oil and gas, and paper and forest industry groups commanded a 29% weighting of the TSE 300 stocks in March 1990. By February 1998 these groups made up only 20.3% of the TSE 300 by weighting.

You hear strange commentary about cyclical stocks on Bay Street, such as "You can make a lot of money on the cyclicals if you get in and out at the right time." That's a big "if." And for everybody who gets in and out at the right time, somebody gets in and out at the wrong time. The idea is that you buy a mining company at $12 and sell it 18 months later at $32, because everybody knows it's going right back down to $12 the minute copper prices start going back down. The trouble is, you never really know if you're getting in at the right time, and nobody ever talks about the guy who bought your cyclical company shares at $32 (somebody had to!). The cyclical stock that goes up for a few years only to fall back to where it started is a zero-sum game. The average investor doesn't make a dime in capital gains, and can only hope for the odd measly dividend payment.

Why don't Canadian cyclical stocks perform well? It's a difficult question to answer, but it appears to be related to a few factors. One is that the prices of the commodities these companies produce rarely remain strong for very long, and have failed to increase over long periods of time. There's hardly ever a serious shortage of most commodities such as copper, nickel, gold, zinc, lumber, pulp, paper, steel, oil, etc. Countries all around the globe produce these products and ship them to wherever there is demand. If there ever is a shortage and the commodity price strengthens, several companies will rush to crank up an idle plant, a new plant, or a recycling facility that makes this stuff, and flood the market with new product that pushes the price of the commodity back down.

Another reason is that resource-based companies are hugely capital intensive. The cost of building a new mine, pulp mill, or steel mill is enormous. It's difficult for a company to accurately predict the cost of building a new facility and ensure that it's profitable once up and running. Further, resource-related companies tend to have above-average labour costs. That's good for the employees, but not as good for shareholders.

Why do people buy cyclical stocks? It's a rare occurrence, but a mining or oil and gas company making a big discovery can drive its share price up very quickly. Some investors are attracted to the above-average volatility of some cyclical stocks, hoping to make a quick killing. And some Canadian pension fund and mutual fund managers buy the resource and cyclical stocks because the law currently requires tax-sheltered investments to stay in Canadian companies, and so they feel compelled to pick up a few resource stocks if they can't find good stock values elsewhere. Fans of gold like to own gold stocks, believing that gold is as good as money and a hedge against inflation and political instability.

And some resource companies, especially the gold miners, seem to have been excused from having to produce increasing long-term profits for shareholders. This makes it easier for gold miners to sell stock, and easier for investors to justify buying such stocks. The gold stocks are largely valued not on earnings, they way most companies are, but on cash flow. This is the amount of money a company brings in before taking into account charges for amortization and depreciation of equipment and major capital outlays in the past (such as building the gold mine in the first place). Why cash flow instead of net income? It's probably because few of the gold miners have any dependable net income to speak of!

There are exceptions to this. For example, Canada's biggest gold miner, Barrick Gold Corp. (ABX-TSE), has low mining costs, a unique "hedging" program that ensures above-average revenues for its gold, and a long history of solid net income. Placer Dome Inc. (PDG-TSE), Canada's second-biggest gold miner, also has a good cost profile but a spottier track record for earnings.

> **A**s an aside to more hands-on investors, it's a good idea to stay away from any company that doesn't have earnings or which the "pros" evaluate in terms of cash flow instead of net income. Stock evaluation techniques that use cash flow or earnings before interest, taxes, depreciation, and amortization (EBITDA) are often euphemistic analyses of companies that never seem to turn a profit.
>
>

A shareholder owns a piece of a company's shareholders' equity (assets minus liabilities), also known as "book value." That's why stocks are called "equities." Over the long term it's the company's earnings or profits, not its cash flow, that cause its equity to rise. For many cash-flow-oriented companies, all too often the no-earnings routine goes on and on to the point where the company's balance sheet turns into a debt-heavy mess with paltry shareholders' equity. This is what happened to television cable operator Rogers Communications Inc. (RCI.B-TSE), a stock that spent much of the 1990s going south.

Sometimes, of course, shares of companies with cash flow and no earnings soar in anticipation of an era of consistent profitability. So let it be. It's never too late to invest in a well-run company with a long track record of steadily increasing earnings. Invest in earnings, not cash flow!

All this doesn't mean Canadian resource companies don't have a future. They most certainly do, and there may even be a day when they become more like "growth" companies, which tend to have a steadier rise in revenue and earnings over the years. In 1997 and 1998 there were signs that some of Canada's big cyclical companies were getting sick and tired of seeing their stock prices going nowhere over the long term. Noranda Inc., for example, sold off its non-mining interests in order to focus on its main mining and smelting operations with a view to increasing the company's earnings. (Noranda shareholders haven't gone totally unrewarded over the years; a reasonable dividend has long been paid.) And in early 1998 Inco Ltd. was talking tough about cutting costs and closing marginally profitable mines. MacMillan Bloedel Ltd. too was taking steps to improve its profitability.

> Eventually there will be a day when the world gets seriously low on non-renewable resources like copper, gold, nickel, oil, and gas, and the prices for these commodities will skyrocket. But it's hard to imagine it will be anytime in the near future. So the long-term investor should tread carefully with cyclical resource stocks, and is probably better off leaving them for the "pros."

NON–CYCLICAL INVESTING: THE TILTED INDEX APPROACH

TIPS investors should note that they own a significant piece of several cyclical or resource stocks. Buying a few stocks of non-cyclical companies in addition to TIPS reduces the overall exposure to cyclical stocks.

A voiding all mining, forest-products, oil and gas, and steel stocks narrows the TSE 300 down to about 180 companies, the TSE 100 to about 68 companies, and the Toronto 35 to just 21 companies, as of March 1998. That makes it quite possible to cost-effectively build and maintain your very own "indexed" portfolio of the Toronto 35 non-cyclical stocks as a long-term investing strategy for your Canadian equity investments. Based on long-term historical returns of Canadian cyclical stocks and the Canadian stock market, this "tilted index" strategy stands a good chance of providing long-term returns above the Toronto 35 and the TSE 300.

This strategy is best executed with a lump sum of money invested all at once in the non-cyclical Toronto 35 stocks. The stocks should be purchased in rough correspondence with their weighting in the index with the resource-stock weightings factored out. Just eyeball it. For example, the February 1998 *Review* shows that min-ing, oil, steel, and forest stocks made up a combined 25% of the Toronto 35 by weighting, leaving the remaining non-cyclical stocks with a 75% weighting. This means you should bump up the weight-ing of the remaining non-cyclical stocks by a factor of about 1.3 (100% divided by 75%), in order to roughly map out your tilted index. If Thomson Corp.'s (TOC-TSE) Toronto 35 weighting is, say, 4%, then make Thomson Corp. 5% or so of your tilted index. For added ease, select just two bank stocks instead of all six, but make their combined weights roughly the same as all of the banks. (There might be only two left anyway by now, at the rate they're merging.)

PUTTING IT INTO PRACTICE

Investors with as little as $20,000 available for the Canadian stock portion of their portfolios can put this strategy to work cost effec-tively, but it's possible with even less money. Buying 20 stocks at

$25 a pop costs $500, or 2.5% of the $20,000 investment. That upfront one-time fee amounts to very little when spread out over many years, and beats even the lowest MER no-load mutual funds hands down on costs over the long term. Investors with more money will find it even more cost-effective, because you'll be dealing with fewer odd lots.

Sound like a lot of work? Don't worry about it. Once started, this approach requires very little maintenance. The stocks will go up and down and roughly maintain their weighting in line with the non-cyclical component of the Toronto 35. Any changes to the Toronto 35 are made but once a year (in February), unless a company gets taken over and must be replaced. Any changes you need to make can be done during the annual checkup of your portfolio, when you sell any stocks that were taken out of the index and buy any new ones that were added. (You don't *have* to sell stocks that get kicked out of the Toronto 35; it just means the stock hasn't kept up with the pack—not that the company is going out of business.)

Dividends combined with new cash to invest can be put towards new purchases every few months or once a year. New money invested in this strategy should be invested in such a way as to keep your portfolio roughly in line with the non-cyclical component of the Toronto 35. Obviously you can't spread out $2,500 of new money over 20 stocks, but you can buy a couple of different Toronto 35 stocks on a rotating basis each time you put new money into the strategy. (Or you can simply buy TIPS to blend the two strategies together.)

Investors just starting out can also gradually build a Canadian stock portfolio that eventually takes on the shape of the non-cyclical component of the Toronto 35.

Investors interested in the Tilted Index approach may want to buy a diversified group of the roughly 68 non-cyclical stocks that make up the TSE 100. While it would be impractical to buy all 68 stocks, you could build a diversified portfolio of 15 to 25 non-cyclical TSE 100 stocks. Any changes would be made just once a year, during the annual checkup. This strategy allows more choice and a decent shot at returns above the TSE 100 and TSE 300.

WORDS TO PICK STOCKS BY

Finally, a few general words about picking Canadian stocks, or any stocks for that matter, for the long term. As you scour the TSE 300 and learn a bit about the various companies, let your common sense guide you to good long-term stock picks. Avoid gimmicky-sounding or faddish products or businesses. Stick with companies that make a product or provide a service that many people need or enjoy and that's likely to be in demand for a very long time. Don't let boring-sounding companies turn you off, and be skeptical of the exciting-sounding ones. And steer clear of the "penny stocks," which are stocks that trade below $5 per share. Penny stocks are often highly speculative or belong to troubled companies.

Remember, the stock market rewards companies that grow bigger over the long term. Also remember that bigger companies (generally the ones with bigger weightings) have more built-in diversification than smaller companies.

Putting It All Together

DIVERSIFYING HERE AND ABROAD

GOING GLOBAL: BUYING FOREIGN STOCKS

Beyond Spiders, Diamonds, and WEBS, there are many ways to diversify your stock holdings internationally with individual stocks. You might want to buy a few individual stocks to round out your Spiders and WEBS holdings, or make up a diversified portfolio of U.S. and other foreign stocks.

The United States provides the easiest and closest-to-home way of diversifying outside Canada. All the discount brokers let you buy U.S. stocks as easily as you buy Canadian stocks, and it usually costs only a few dollars more.

We've mentioned many of the big U.S. companies already, many of which are household names. The United States has a long list of stocks that are ideal "buy-and-hold" candidates, because there are far more large, multinational companies there than here (or in any other country, for that matter). The U.S. stocks named in the Index Stocks chapter and elsewhere in this book provide you with enough information to pick just a few U.S. stocks or to build a complete diversified portfolio.

Just as you build a Canadian-stock portfolio by sticking only with TSE 300 stocks, you can build a U.S. stock portfolio by holding S&P 500 stocks only. If one of your stocks gets kicked out of these indexes, then you should consider selling them. To find out what stocks make up the S&P 500, order an up-to-date Spiders prospectus. Or for those with Internet access, check out www.standardandpoors.com, a handy website that lists the 500 stocks both alphabetically and by industry.

Some of the discount brokers also offer trading of securities listed on stock exchanges abroad—in Europe and Asia, for example. This opens up a world of opportunities. Commissions for this type of trading, however, are high, often in the hundreds of dollars per trade—so buying stocks on foreign exchanges is uneconomical for most small investors.

FOREIGN STOCKS ON THE NYSE

A much cheaper route to international stock investing outside North America is the New York Stock Exchange, which lists the shares of hundreds of foreign companies, mostly through American Depositary Receipts, or ADRs.

> ADRs are NYSE-traded shares of large non-U.S. companies based in Europe, Latin America, Asia (including China), and elsewhere. You can buy an ADR just as you would buy a U.S. stock, with the same commission.

ADRs allow small investors a cost-effective way of reaching into parts of the world not even covered by WEBS. You could buy a diversified handful of companies based in emerging economies such as Latin America, China, and even Russia, for example, as a substitute for an emerging-markets mutual fund. Canadian mutual funds that invest in Latin America and emerging markets typically have MERs in the high 2% range, often well above 3%! Buying your own international stocks is a far cheaper alternative.

> **K**eep in mind that investing in emerging markets is risky business, whether you buy stocks or mutual funds. The rewards can be high, and so can the losses. Your investment is affected by currency exchange rates as well as by business conditions in the chosen country. Allow for significant volatility in shares of companies in developing nations. And keep such investments to a small portion of your portfolio, say between 10% to 20%.

Dividends paid by foreign-company shares are treated as income for Canadian tax purposes, and taxes are likely to be withheld by the company's country. Canada has tax treaties with many developed countries, which limits their tax withholding to 15%. A tax credit is generally available on your Canadian tax return.

> **B**elow are some foreign companies that trade on the NYSE. (For a complete list, contact the NYSE at 212-656-3000 and request an up-to-date list of ADRs. Or check out www.bankofny.com/adr on the World Wide Web, set up by Bank of New York.

This first list contains some of the NYSE-listed foreign companies based in WEBS-covered countries. When looking for foreign stocks, note that telecommunications stocks and bank stocks usually make good proxies for the country's stock market, just as BCE Inc. and the Canadian banks are highly representative of the Canadian stock market.

Australia:
News Corp. (NWS) — International media.

France:
Alcatel Alsthom (ALA) — Telecommunications, energy.
France Telecom (FTE) — Telecommunications.
Rhone-Poulenc S.A. (RP) — Drugs, chemicals.
SGS-THOMSON (STM) — Circuits, electronics.

Germany:
Daimler-Benz AG (DAI) — Automobiles.
Deutsche Telekom AG (DT) — Telecommunications.
Hoechst AG (HOE) — Chemicals.

Hong Kong:
APT Satellite Holdings Ltd. (ATS) — Satellite services.
China Telecom (Hong Kong) Ltd. (CHL) — Telecommunications.
China Tire Holdings Ltd. (TIR) — Tires.
Hong Kong Telecommunications Ltd. (HKT) — Telecommunications.

Italy:
Fiat S.p.A. (FIA) — Automobiles.
Telecom Italia S.p.A. (TI) — Telecommunications.

Japan:
Hitachi Ltd. (HIT) — Electronics, machinery.
Honda Motor Co. (HMC) — Automobiles, motorcycles.
Matsushita Electric Industrial Co. (MC) — Electronics.
Nippon Telegraph and Telephone Corp. (NTT) — Telecommunications.
Pioneer Electronic Corp. (PIO) — Electronics.
Sony Corp. (SNE) — Electronics, entertainment.
TDK Corp. (TDK) — Electronics.

Mexico:
Coca-Cola FEMSA, S.A. (KOF) — Bottling, soft drinks.
Desc, S.A. (DES) — Manufacturing, financial services.
Grupo Casa Autrey S.A. (ATY) — Pharmaceuticals, foods.
Grupo Financiero Serfin S.A. (SFN) — Financial services.
Grupo Industrial Maseca S.A. (MSK) — Corn flour.
Grupo Iusacell S.A. (CEL) — Wireless telecommunications.
Grupo Televisa S.A. (TV) — Media.
Pepsi-Gemex S.A. (GEM) — Bottling.
Telefonos de Mexico S.A. (TMX) — Phone company.
Vitro S.A. (VTO) — Glass.

Netherlands:
ABN AMRO Holding N.V. (AAN) — Banking, financial services.
Elsevier NV (ENL) — Publishing.
ING Groep N.V. (ING) — Financial services.
KLM Royal Dutch Airlines (KLM) — Airline.
Philips Electronics N.V. (PHG) — Electronics.
PolyGram N.V. (PLG) — Entertainment.
Royal Dutch Petroleum Co. (RD) — Oil and gas.
Unilever N.V. (UN) — Foods, consumer products.

Spain:
ARGENTARIA-Corporacion Bancaria de Espana S.A. (AGR) — Banking.
Banco Bilbao Vizcaya S.A. (BBV) — Banking.
Banco Central Hispanoamericano S.A. (BCH) — Banking.
Banco de Santander S.A. (STD) — Banking.
Endesa S.A. (ELE) — Electric utility.
Telefonica de Espana S.A. (TEF) — Telephone company.

Sweden:
Astra AB (A), (AAB) — Drugs.
Scania AB (SCVA), (SCVB) — Heavy vehicles.

United Kingdom:
Barclays Bank PLC (BCS) — Banking.
Bass Public Ltd. (BAS) — Beer, hotels.
British Airways Plc (BAB) — Airline.
British Petroleum Co. (BP) — Oil and gas.
British Sky Broadcasting Group Plc (BSY) — Broadcasting.
British Telecommunications Plc (BTY) — Telecommunications.
Cable & Wireless Plc (BTY) — Telecommunications.
Cadbury Schweppes plc (CSG) — Beverages, candy.
Glaxo Wellcome plc (GLX) — Drugs.
Saatchi & Saatchi PLC (SSA) — Marketing communications.
SmithKline Beecham plc (SBH) — Drugs.
Unilever PLC (UL) — Food, consumer products.

The following list contains NYSE-listed foreign companies based in countries not currently covered by WEBS.

ARGENTINA

BAESA-Buenos Aires Embotelladora, SA (BAE) — Bottling.
Banco Frances del Rio de la Plata, S.A. (BFR) — Banking.
Banco Rio de la Plata S.A. (BRS) — Banking.
DISCO S.A. (DXO) — Food Retailing.
IRSA-Inversiones y Representaciones, S.A. (IRS) — Real Estate.
MetroGas, S.A. (MGS) — Gas Distribution.
Nortel Inversora S.A. (NTL) — Telecom.
Quilmes Industrial, Societe Anonyme (LQU) — Beer.
Telecom Argentina STET-France Telecom S.A. (TEO) — Telecom.
Telefonica de Argentina S.A. (TAR) — Telecom.
Transportadora de Gas del Sur S.A. (TGS) — Gas Transportation.
YPF Sociedad Anonima (YPF) — Oil and Gas Exploration.

BAHAMAS (non-ADRs)

Sun International Hotels Ltd. (SIH) — Resorts.
Teekay Shipping Corp. (TK) — Oil, Petroleum Transportation.

BRAZIL

Aracruz Celulose S.A. (ARA) — Pulp & Paper.
Companhia Brasileira de Distribuicao (ARA) — Food Retailing.
Companhia Cervejaria Brahma (BRH) — Beer.
Companhia Paranaense de Energia-COPEL (ELP) — Electricity.
Companhia Siderugica Nacional (SID) — Steel.
Telecommunicacoes Brasileiras S.A.-Telebras (TBR) — Telecom.
Uniao de Bancos Brasileiros S.A. (UBB) — Banking.

CHILE

Administradora de Fondos de Pensiones-Provida S.A. (PVD) —
    Pension-Fund Administration.
Banco BHIF (BB) — Banking.
Banco de A. Edwards (AED) — Banking.
Banco Santiago (SAN) — Banking.
Banco Santander-Chile (BSB) — Banking.
Chilgener S.A. (CHR) — Electricity.

Compania de Telecomunicaciones de Chile S.A. (CTC) — Telecom.
Cristalerias de Chile S.A. (CGW) — Glass Manufacture.
Distribucion y Servicio D&S S.A. (DYS) — Supermarkets.
Embotelladora Andina S.A. (AKOA/AKOB) — Coca-Cola Production.
Empresa Nacional de Electricidad S.A. (EOC) — Electricity.
Empresas Telex-Chila S.A. (TL) — Telecom.
Enersis S.A. (ENI) — Electricity.
Laboratorio Chile S.A. (LBC) — Pharmaceuticals.
Linea Aerea Nacional Chile S.A. (LFL) — Airline.
Madeco S.A. (MAD) — Telecom/Industrial.
MASISA-Maderas y Sinteticos Sociedad Anonima (MYS) — Wood
    Products.
QUINENCO S.A. (LQ) — Diversified Industrial/Financial Services.
Santa Isabel S.A. (ISA) — Supermarkets.
SQM-Sociedad Quimica y Minera de Chile S.A. (SQM) — Chemicals.
Supermercados Unimarc S.A. (UNR) — Retail, Supermarkets.
Vina Concha y Toro, S.A. (VCO) — Wine.

CHINA
Beijing Yanhua Petrochemical Co. (BYH) — Petrochemicals.
China Eastern Airlines Corp. (CEA) — Airline.
China Southern Airlines Co. (ZNH) — Airline.
Guangshen Railway Co. (GSH) — Rail Transportation.
Huaneng Power International Inc. (HNP) — Power Plants.
Jilin Chemical Industrial Co. (JCC) — Chemicals.
Shandong Huaneng Power Development Co. (SH) — Electricity.
Shanghai Petrochemical Co. (SHI) — Petrochemicals.

COLOMBIA
Banco Ganadero S.A. (BGA) — Banking.
Banco Industrial Colombiano S.A. (CIB) — Banking.

DENMARK
Novo-Nordisk A/S (NVO) — Pharmaceuticals.
Tele Danmark A/S (TLD) — Telecom.

FINLAND
Nokia Corp. (NOKA) — Telecom/Electronics.

GHANA
Ashanti Goldfields Co. (ASL) — Gold Mining.

HONG KONG/China
Amway Asia Pacific Ltd. (AAP) — Amway Distribution.
APT Satellite Holdings Ltd. (ATS) — Satellite Services.
Asia Satellite Telecommunications Holdings Ltd. (SAT) — Satellite Transponder.
Brilliance China Automotive Holdings Ltd. (CBA) — Automotive.
China Telecom (Hong Kong) Ltd. (CHL) — Telecom.
China Tire Holdings Ltd. (TIR) — Tires.
Ek Chor China Motorcycle Co. (EKC) — Motorcycles.
Hong Kong Telecommunications Ltd. (HKT) — Telecom.
Tommy Hilfiger Corp. (TOM) — Clothes.

HUNGARY
Magyar Tavkozlesi Tr. (MTA) — Telecom.

INDONESIA
Gulf Indonesia Resources Ltd. (GRL).
Indonesian Satellite Corp. (IIT) — Telecom.
P.T. Telekomunikasi Indonesia (TLK) — Telecom.
P.T. TriPolyta Indonesia (TPI) — Polypropylene.

IRELAND
Allied Irish Banks P.L.C. (AIB) — Banking.
Elan Corp. plc (ELN) — Pharmaceuticals.
Governor and Co. of the Bank of Ireland (IRE) — Banking.
Jefferson Smufit Group plc (JS) — Paper, Packaging.

ISRAEL
Blue Square-Israel Ltd. (BSI) — Retail, Supermarkets.
Elscint Ltd. (ELT) — Medical Technology.
Koor Industries Ltd. (KOR) — Telecom.
Super-Sol Ltd. (SAE) — Supermarkets.
Tadiran Ltd. (TAD) — Telecom.
Tefron Ltd. (TFR) — Clothes.

KOREA
Korea Electric Power Corp. (KEP) — Utility.
KS Telecom Co (SKM) — Telecom.
Pohang Iron & Steel Co. (PKX) — Steel.

LIBERIA
Royal Caribbean Cruises Ltd. — (RCL).

LUXEMBOURG
Espirito Santo Financial Group S.A. (ESF) — Financial Services.

NETHERLANDS ANTILLES
Schlumberger Ltd. (SLB) — Oil & Gas Services, Electronics.
Singer Co. N.V. (SEW) — Sewing Machines.

NEW ZEALAND
Fletcher Challenge Ltd. (FFS) — Forest Products.
Fletcher Challenge Building (FLB) — Construction Materials.
Fletcher Challenge Energy (FEG) — Oil & Gas.
Fletcher Challenge Paper (FLP) — Pulp & Paper.
Telecom Corp. of New Zealand Ltd. (NZT) — Telecom.

NORWAY
Norsk Hydro A.S. (NHY) — Natural Source Products.
Petroleum Geo-Services ASA (PGO) — Oil Services.
Saga Petroleum a.s. (SPMA/SPMB) — Oil & Gas Exploration.
Smedvig asa (SMBA/SMVB) — Offshore Oil Drilling.

PANAMA
Banco Latinoamericano de Exportaciones S.A. (BLX) — Banking.
Panamerican Beverages Inc. (PB) — Bottling.
Willbros Group Inc. (WG) — Construction/Engineering.

PERU
Banco Wiese Limitado (BWP) — Banking.
Compania de Minas Buenaventura S.A. (BVN) — Mining.
Credicorp LTd. (BAP) — Financial Services.
Telefonica del Peru S.A. (TDP) — Telecom.

PHILIPPINES
Benguet Corp. (BE) — Mining.
Philippines Long Distance Telephone co. (PHI) — Telecom.

PORTUGAL
Banco Comercial Portugues S.A. (BPC) — Banking.
Electricidade de Portugal S.A. (EDP) — Electricity.
Portugal Telecom S.A. (PT) — Telecom.

RUSSIA
OAO Rostelecom (ROS) — Telecom.
Vimpel-Communications (VIP) — Telecom.

SOUTH AFRICA
ASA Ltd. (ASA) — Investments.

TAIWAN
Taiwan Semiconductor Manufacturing Co. (TSM) — Semiconductors.

VENEZUELA
Compania Anonima Nacional Telfonos de Venezuela (VNT) —
    Telecom.
Corimon C.A. (CRM) — Industrial Management.
Mavesa S.A. (MAV) — Food, Household Items.

BUILDING A DIVERSIFIED
CANADIAN BOND PORTFOLIO

Despite the huge popularity of mutual funds, many Canadians are
still buying GICs and Canada Savings Bonds. These investors
haven't been convinced that the stock market is a secure enough
place to put their money. They're far happier and they sleep better
at night knowing that their investments are guaranteed.

> It's fine to stay away from stocks if you're looking for secure, low-risk
> investments. But GIC and CSB investors should take note: Canadian
> government bonds usually offer higher returns with no added risk.

Just like buying your own stocks, buying your own bonds is a superior route compared with mutual funds. Buying your own bonds is a piece of cake, and you will completely sidestep the 1.59% average MER that Canadian bond funds charged in 1997.

Bond fund MERs act as a drag on your bond returns. If the current yield on a 30-year Canadian government bond that you own directly is 6%, that's the annual return you will get if you hold the bond until it matures (and as long as the government doesn't go broke!). If the average yield on a bunch of bonds in a bond fund is 6%, the fund investor gets 6% minus roughly whatever the MER is. Of course, the average yield in the bond fund will move around all the time as the fund buys and sells bonds, but the point is you're forever getting clipped by more than a full percentage point every year that you're in a bond fund. If you're in a bond fund with an average yield of 6% and an MER of 1.5%, you're coughing up about 25% of your income every year!

There are no "commissions" per se when you buy bonds from a discount broker, but the discount broker does make money. This is because the bond price will be marked up a little bit when the bond is sold to you. It's difficult to get a good handle on how much mark-up the discount brokers charge, because Canada's bond market isn't as transparent as the stock market. Unlike the stock market, the prices that the big financial institutions are paying for bonds aren't posted for everyone to see, and the discount brokers don't generally disclose their bond mark-ups. Having said this, based on a quick investigation into discount broker bond trading it appears that discount brokers' mark-ups on bonds are quite small, and shouldn't be considered a deterrent against buying bonds from discount brokers. The adverse effect of the mark-up is much less than the adverse effect of bond fund MERs.

Buying your own bonds from a discount broker is even easier than buying stocks. When you call the discount broker to buy a bond you will be connected with a representative who will take your order. Your job is to tell the representative what type of bond you want to buy, and what maturity. The representative will tell you the price and yield of the bond, and how much you'll need to buy it. One way to make sure you're getting a good deal on your bond is to check in the latest newspaper for the yield on the bond you're looking to buy. For example, the newspaper may indicate that a Province of Ontario bond maturing in 2020 has a yield of 6.0%, while the representative quotes you a yield of 5.95% for the same bond. That's a minor difference.

> **I**f the yield the representative quotes you is much different from the yield in the newspaper, ask why. Feel free to ask for several quotes on different bonds of different maturities.

It's easy to stay diversified when buying bonds because interest rates and bond yields are constantly changing. To diversify further, a bond investor should be sure to stagger maturities, perhaps by buying some long-term bonds that mature 25 years or so from the time of purchase, some that mature in 10 or 15 years, and some that mature in five years or less. Staggering the bond maturities reduces interest-rate risk.

> **G**enerally speaking, however, younger investors saving for retirement should lean towards buying more long-term bonds than short-term bonds, since long-term yields are usually higher. The further out in the future that a bond matures, the higher annual yield it usually offers.

CANADIAN FEDERAL AND PROVINCIAL GOVERNMENT BONDS

The simplest and safest way to buy bonds for your RRSP is to stick with those issued by the federal government of Canada (Canadian bonds) or by the provinces (provincial bonds). Provincial bonds are also issued by provincially owned companies such as Ontario Hydro and Quebec Hydro.

> **A**ll Canadian and provincial bonds are guaranteed by the governments that issue them, which means they'll pay you back your interest and principal if it's the last thing they do.
> ⊙———

Provincial bonds usually offer a higher yield than Canadian bonds, which makes them ideal for do-it-yourself investors. The reason for higher provincial yields is ostensibly because there's a bit more risk in owning a provincial bond, but this added risk is minimal. Can you imagine if Prince Edward Island or Saskatchewan ran into financial difficulty one day, and the rest of the country didn't help out? That wouldn't be Canada as we know it.

Here are some examples.

On March 16, 1998, you had your choice of the following bonds:

Issuer	Coupon	Maturity	Price	Yield
Canada	8.75%	Dec 2005	121.401	5.325%
Canada	10.25%	Mar 2014	148.885	5.587%
Canada	9.00%	Jun 2025	144.499	5.745%
Alberta	7.50%	Dec 2005	113.034	5.407%
B.C.	8.00%	Aug 2005	115.219	5.479%
Newflnd	10.13%	Nov 2014	143.003	6.006%
Ontario	8.00%	Jun 2026	126.234	6.049%
Saskatchwn	8.75%	May 2025	136.175	6.027%

The price is per one hundred dollars of the face amount of the bond, which the bondholder receives when the bond matures. The indicated coupon rate multiplied by the face amount is the amount the bond pays in interest per year.

Note how you could have had a 2005 bond from Alberta or British Columbia with a significantly higher yield than a 2005 Canada bond. Unless you think there's a chance B.C. or Alberta won't keep good on the promise to pay you your interest and principal, why not go with their bonds?

See how the yield on the Newfoundland 2014 bond is much greater than the Canada 2014 bond yield. And look at the extra yield you get by buying the Ontario or Saskatchewan bond over the Canada 2025 bond. The difference in yield makes for a whole lot of extra dough over the years.

> With province of Quebec or Quebec Hydro bonds you can sometimes get even higher yields, but you must be prepared for possible volatility in the bond price whenever the separatist movement turns up the heat. (Every time the Quebec separatist thing hits the foreign newspapers, foreigners sell Canadian and Quebec bonds because they think the sky is falling.) And you have to have faith that Quebec or Quebec Hydro will repay you.

When buying bonds from most discount brokers, you're looking at a minimum investment of $5,000 for the face value of the bond. Remember that the face value is the amount you're paid back when the bond matures. The actual amount you must hand over when buying a bond depends on its price. To calculate the amount, take the price and divide it by 100; then take that number and multiply it by $5,000, or whatever minimum your discount broker sets for bond trading. In the case of the Alberta bond above, you're looking at a minimum investment of about (113.034/100) × $5,000 = $5,651.7.

The minimum $5,000 face value might strike some as too high for making regular purchases of small amounts of bonds. Consider strip bonds, as discussed below, or consider buying a bond for your entire RRSP contribution once every few years.

ZERO-COUPON OR "STRIP" BONDS

Strip bonds are available for government of Canada and provincial bonds. Strip bonds don't make regular interest payments the way ordinary bonds do. Instead, they're sold at a big discount to their face value, and gradually rise to the face value at the time of maturity. Some bond investors may find this a convenient advantage, since there's no worrying about reinvesting any interest payments.

Others may prefer to get regular interest payments (for income, or just to have more cash to invest in stocks or whatever).

It's mainly a personal choice, but note that strip bonds are less liquid (harder to sell) than regular bonds; their prices are more volatile too. Further, a strip bond's entire return is considered interest for tax purposes, which means the favourable taxation of capital gains is lost with strip bonds purchased outside an RRSP.

> Investors with small amounts of money will find buying strip bonds easier than buying regular bonds. You can buy strip bonds with as little as $1,000 or even less sometimes, depending on the maturity date and the availability of such bonds at the discount broker.

REAL RETURN BONDS

Another type of Canadian government bond is a real return bond, which takes inflation into account when providing returns for the holder. A bond's real return is its return minus the prevailing rate of inflation. High inflation is bad for bond prices (since inflation reduces the buying power of money). Real return bonds ensure the bondholder gets returns above the rate of inflation, if inflation is high. But these bonds don't necessarily provide better returns if inflation is low, or negative. That's why, if you decide on real return bonds, you should be sure to have a few regular bonds as well.

If all this bond stuff confuses you, don't worry. Your discount broker will help you get the right bond. Just explain how much you have to invest, and know ahead of time roughly what maturity date you're looking for and whether you want a government of Canada bond or a provincial bond. You can scan the daily bond quotes in a good business paper to get an idea of what you want.

CORPORATE BONDS

For the slightly more daring investor seeking even higher yields than Canadian or provincial bonds, there are always corporate bonds. Here you're getting riskier, because a company is more likely to go bust than a government. Still, you might find it worthwhile to buy bonds from solid companies, such as the big banks or utilities, that you feel certain will be around long enough to pay you back. Corporate bonds can be purchased for as little as the $5,000 face value at most discount brokers.

To find out which corporate bonds exist, simply look in the newspaper where all the market data is. You'll see corporate bonds issued by many of the companies listed on the TSE, such as Bell Canada (BCE), Bombardier, Canadian Utilities, Westcoast Energy, Royal Bank, and Thomson.

If you do decide to buy corporate bonds, be sure to practise diversification. If you put a lot of your bond investments on one company, it could demolish your savings if the company is unable to pay you back. Be sure to buy bonds issued by different companies.

Beyond solid corporate bonds there are high-yield bonds, also known as junk bonds. These are issued by companies with mediocre or poor credit ratings, and are for the experienced, highly risk-tolerant investor only. The high-yield bond market is an area where a bond fund with a low MER starts to make good sense, since the yields ought to be significantly higher than government bonds or solid corporate bonds, and the risk is lowered by spreading it out over many different bonds. If you invest in a high-yield fund, however, keep it to a small to moderate portion of your bond investments. There's no guarantee that these funds will outperform government bonds.

That's all for buying bonds. Remember that there's no need to turn yourself into a bond trader. If you've decided to buy a bond, just sit back and let it mature or sell it only when you need the money.

> If, however, you really think you know which way interest rates are headed, then be my guest and become a bond trader. If your crystal ball tells you that interest rates are going to go up, you should sell all your bonds and buy them back when interest rates plateau. If you're sure interest rates are about to go down, buy bonds. It's that simple. Countless people spend their days trying to predict the future of interest rates, and countless people fail to get it right.

The Gambler

Let's face it, many people have a bit of the gambling bug in them. They must, or there wouldn't be billions, if not trillions, of dollars' worth of stocks and bonds flying back and forth each day around the world.

As if buying stocks weren't risky or volatile enough, there's a whole host of other investment techniques that can earn you—or lose you—a lot of money in a very short time. This includes things like options, buying on margin, and buying speculative stocks.

The easiest way to approach these investment techniques is... to avoid them entirely! The sober investor seeking to outperform the average mutual fund is far better off skipping this brief chapter, and moving on to the next.

However, for those who feel compelled to speculate with a small amount of your money, here are a few ideas.

First off, limit your gambling money to a fraction of your savings. If you're young, it might be 10%. If you're older and have dependants, better make it 5% or less. Be prepared to lose much or all of the money you set aside for gambling.

If you do lose all your gambling money, quit gambling. If you make money and still want to gamble, then use only those profits. Don't ever start thinking you're on some hot streak, and start gambling with your savings. You'll regret it.

The following is a list of ways to gamble in the capital markets, ranked more or less in rising order of riskiness.

THE "MARKET TIMER"

This means making periodic predictions about the near-term future of a stock or an overall stock market. You decide when it's "a good time to get in the market" and when it's "time to get out." The masses who toil in the world's financial markets are mostly market timers. This is why several hundred million shares change hands on the bigger stock exchanges every day, even on slow days.

One form of market timing is the "Sell It and Buy It Right Back" approach. This classic gambling method involves selling an investment with every intention of buying it back shortly at a lower price. For example, you sell your WEBS Spain index stock at $30 per share because you read that the Basque separatists have bombed a post office in Barcelona, and you plan to buy the index stock back at $26 as investors panic over the coming Second Spanish Civil War. Or you sell your 50 shares of Geac Computer Corp. (GAC-TSE) at $56 because you know, you just know, that the stock is about to tumble, and you have every intention of buying it back at $48 a week from now. Watch those commissions and the tax collector.

SPLIT SHARES

Buying split shares is actually an easy way to add some pizzazz to an investment portfolio, but it's still quite risky. On certain big-company Canadian stocks, such as the banks and the telephone companies, you can buy split shares. These inventions take the common shares of one or more companies and divide them into two "split" shares.

One set of the split shares is usually called the "capital" shares and the other is the "preferred." All of the dividends of the underlying stock go to the preferred split shares, while all of the capital gains of the underlying stock go to the capital split shares. The result is that the preferred split holders get solid, dependable dividends on a secure investment that acts more like a bond than a stock. And the capital split holders get a "leveraged" play on the underlying stock, which means their investment will fluctuate much more than the underlying stock. The preferred split shares are low-risk; the capital split shares carry much more risk. ⊙——

There are several split shares available at any given time. For example, Telco Split Corp. operates a set of preferred split shares (TSC.PR.A-TSE) and a set of capital split shares (TSC-TSE) incorporating several of Canada's major telephone companies: BCE Inc. (B-TSE), Telus Corp. (AGT-TSE), Manitoba Telecom Services Inc. (MBT-TSE), BC Telecom Inc. (BCT-TSE), NewTel Enterprises Ltd. (NEL-TSE), Quebectel Group Inc. (QTG-TSE), Maritime Telegraph and Telephone Co. (MTT-TSE), and Bruncor Inc. (BRR-TSE).

Like most split shares, the Telco preferred shares are very stable and provide dividend income, while the Telco capital shares are volatile and provide leveraged returns. An example in the Telco Split Corp. prospectus shows that if the above stocks returned 11.5% on average per year from August 1997 to August 2002, the Telco capital shares would return 17.6% per year. Conversely, if the above stocks fell in value, the Telco capital shares would fall even more in value. Note that, like all split shares, the Telco split shares have a time limit. The Telco split shares will be redeemed on Sept. 1, 2002 by Telco Split Corp.

Another split share offering is Allbanc Split Corp., which operates preferred and capital split shares incorporating the top five Canadian banks: Royal Bank of Canada (RY-TSE), Bank of Montreal (BMO-TSE), Canadian Imperial Bank of Commerce (CM-TSE), Toronto-Dominion Bank (TD-TSE), and Bank of Nova Scotia (BNS-TSE).

Telco Split (416-862-5842) and Allbanc Split are affiliated with ScotiaMcLeod Inc., a securities firm. They also offer split shares on BCE Inc. alone and Bank of Nova Scotia alone. Call for a prospectus.

Pipe NT Corp. also offers preferred (PIP.PR.A) and capital (PIP-TSE) split shares on the Canadian pipeline companies: TransCanada PipeLines Inc. (TRP-TSE), Westcoast Energy Inc. (W-TSE), and Enbridge Inc. (ENB-TSE). For information call Pipe NT at 416-359-4000.

Yet another split share is offered by MCM Split Share Corp., which invests in a group of stocks included in the TSE 300 and the S&P 100. Call 416-681-3900 for information.

> One advantage of split shares is diversification in a single investment. But don't forget that it's leveraged diversification; if you hold the capital shares your investment will go up or down much more than the underlying stocks. The preferred shares, on the other hand, are a lot like any other preferred share. Also note that, like mutual funds, split shares have operating expenses; though usually minor, these affect your returns.

BUYING "ON MARGIN"

Buying on margin, another type of leveraged investment, is buying a stock but only paying for part of it because you get a loan from your broker to cover the rest. Then the stock goes down, the phone rings, and it's your broker asking you for another $1,500 to maintain your position. You don't have another $1,500, so you must sell the stock and take the loss.

The advantage to borrowing money that you use for investments is that the cost of borrowing is tax deductible. The disadvantage is that if the investment works against you, you'll not only have an investment loss but you'll be paying interest costs on top of that.

In recent years, some of Canada's seminar-circuit investment advisors have been urging Canadians to mortgage their homes and use the borrowed proceeds to invest in mutual funds. This is questionable advice, and investors should be well aware of the risks. Mortgaging your home to invest in the stock market is virtually the same as buying stock on margin. A home is not just a place to live;

it's an investment. Why buy a home in the first place and spend years paying off the mortgage if you're just going to mortgage it again and buy mutual funds?

SHORT SELLING

Short selling is betting that a stock will go down, not up. Short selling involves selling the stock before you buy it. You borrow 100 shares of stock from your broker, sell it on the market, wait until the stock plummets, then "cover" the short position by buying back 100 shares at a lower price on the market. You give back the borrowed 100 shares and pocket the amount by which the stock fell. Some, but not all, of the discount brokers will let you sell a stock short.

Top guns on Bay Street have made truckloads full of money using this technique. The successful ones, however, are rabid researchers of companies with high stock valuations, half-baked business plans, or serious problems brewing in their business operations. And the "shorts," as short sellers are often called, are sometimes associated with organized efforts to make disparaging public comments about the company in question, in the hopes that business journalists will write bad things about the company and the word will spread. Very often, the "shorts" turn out to be right.

B ut if you're shorting a stock you must have your finger on the trigger at all times, ready to cover your position, because there's no limit to the amount of money you can lose if the stock goes up instead of down. If you're "long" a stock, meaning you simply own it, the most you can lose is all of your investment. If you're "short," the sky's the limit for potential losses because a stock can go up forever.

SPECULATIVE STOCKS

Speculative stocks are those that aren't part of any major stock index; they usually belong to small, start-up companies with no established record of sales and earnings. The stocks are often called "penny stocks," and the company often has little more than an idea or a product under development and a fast-talking president (who has an even faster-talking team of stock-promoting salespeople). The Vancouver Stock Exchange and the Alberta Stock Exchange are loaded with speculative stocks, but there are lots of them on the Toronto Stock Exchange as well.

This category of gambling can also be called "The Tip," "The Flier," or the "The So-and-So Knows So-and-So Who Works at the Company." People buy these stocks usually because Uncle Horace or someone they know has recommended the stock for whatever reason; investors hope to double, triple, or quintuple their money in a short period of time. Go ahead; buy that chain of poodle salons, the laser-tag thingy, Perpetual Motion Machine Corp., the anti-aging pill maker, or the prosthetic forehead concern.

Go ahead, buy 100 shares of Electronic Abacus Industries Ltd. or Dutch Tulip Bulbs Corp., just because cousin Randy's best friend's hairdresser knew a guy who used to work at the company and the word is it's on the verge of great things. Pick up some shares of that little pharmaceutical company because your friend from university heard that the judge is going to rule in its favour over that nasty patent infringement dispute. Good luck. You'll need it.

JUNIOR MINING STOCKS

So-called "junior" mining stocks are so common in Canada that they deserve their own gambling category. The stock pages, especially the ones that pertain to the Vancouver Stock Exchange and the Alberta Stock Exchange, are loaded with junior mining and oil and gas companies that have nothing but a few bucks in the till and a piece of paper that says they're allowed to go looking for minerals or oil on a piece of property in some exotic-sounding place (read: Bre-X). Thousands of these companies run out of money before finding anything, fold up their tents, and blow away like tumbleweeds in the desert without a single newspaper article ever getting written about them.

The people who run these companies somehow manage to sell their shares just at the right time before everything falls apart (read: Bre-X). Often there are as many people promoting the company to unsuspecting investors as there are geologists actually looking for gold or oil (read: Bre-X). The very, very odd one of these companies hits the jackpot, the shares go absolutely haywire, it's all over the newspapers, and legions of onlookers vow never to pass on the next junior mining "tip" they get.

OPTIONS AND FUTURES

You can also buy a call option or a put option on a stock. An option gives you the right to buy or sell a stock at a set price until the option's expiry date. A call option gives you the right to buy a stock at a set price, and a put option gives you the right to sell a stock at a set price.

If you buy a call option on a stock and the stock goes up a little bit, your call option goes up a lot. If you buy a put option on a stock and the stock goes down a little bit, your put option goes up a lot. If you buy an option and the stock has gone the wrong way come the expiry date, you lose all of your investment!

That's why options are extremely risky. Options give you a shot at tremendously large and quick returns, and the very distinct possibility of losing all of your investment in a hurry. Some advanced or institutional investors use options as a "hedge" to reduce the risk of another investment, but this is an unnecessary tactic for the small investor.

Futures are contracts that require you to buy or sell a commodity at a set price at a set time in the future. Futures are more commonly associated with commodities such as grains, livestock, metals, lumber, and orange juice than they are with the stock market. They're normally used by companies or people who want to lock in the future selling price of their product, but some people use futures to speculate.

I f you want to learn more about options and futures, you're on your own. Wise investors steer clear of them.

Keeping It Straight

TAXES, RECORD-KEEPING, AND SPECIAL SITUATIONS

TAX AND ACCOUNTING TIPS AND STRATEGIES

Whether you invest in mutual funds or index stocks and individual stocks, staying organized is very important and can save you time and headaches down the road.

Some investors think it's easier to stick with mutual funds because at tax time the mutual fund company mails a T5 information slip showing your annual income, dividends, capital gains distributions, and foreign income. Discount brokers track all this stuff for you as well, and mail it to you in the T5 every year.

Do-it-yourself investors, however, must be sure to keep track of capital gains and losses for investments made outside the RRSP.

KEEPING TRACK

Keeping a log of all of your investments, especially the ones made outside the RRSP, is an easy way for the do-it-yourself investor to stay organized. A log comes in handy when doing the annual checkup on your portfolio and at tax time. Buy yourself a nice big book or pad with lined pages. Here you will enter every trade you make, including the stock or bond you bought or sold, the number of shares, the price, the amount of money invested or sold, the commission, the date of the trade, and whether it was done inside or outside the RRSP.

Include any other relevant information you wish. If you're buying or selling a stock in a foreign currency, try to note from the newspaper the exchange rate with the Canadian dollar on the day you did the transaction. This is mainly for back-up purposes, since the transaction slip you receive in the mail after doing a trade should include the Canadian-dollar value of the trade and the exchange rate. Log those figures as well.

Another thing you'll need is a secure place to put your log and your monthly or quarterly statements from your discount broker. Save everything your discount broker mails you! A filing cabinet is best. You want your financial statements to be secure because if you lose them it could turn into a big headache. Trying to find out the purchase price of a stock you bought 14 years ago, for example, can be a big waste of time at tax time.

Your RRSP trading is hassle-free, since there are no tax implications as long as the investments remain inside the RRSP. It's still useful to log your RRSP investments for reference purposes.

INCOME AND DIVIDENDS

Your monthly or quarterly financial statements will show you your interest income and your dividend income paid during the month or quarter and year-to-date, separated by Canadian and U.S. dollars.

At the end of the year you will be mailed a T5 tax slip showing the year's interest income and dividend income. Any amount of foreign income, dividends, or taxes paid to a foreign country during a year will be calculated in Canadian dollars and included in the T5. For cross-checking purposes, some investors might want to note the exchange rate on the day of such payments.

Canadian-dollar interest income is taxed as income. Canadian-company dividends benefit from the dividend tax credit. Foreign income and dividends are taxed as income. Foreign countries usually withhold a percentage of any dividends issued to Canadian stockholders and you can usually receive a federal foreign tax credit for taxes withheld by countries where you have invested. This tax credit is calculated on Schedule 1, Method B of your tax return, in the Federal Tax Calculation. The full amount of any foreign dividends should be included in the "income from foreign sources" section of Schedule 4 of the tax return.

CAPITAL GAINS AND LOSSES

Any time you sell an investment outside the RRSP for a profit or a loss, the profit is a capital gain and the loss is a capital loss. Commissions paid for the purchase and sale of a stock may be included in the calculation to reduce the gain or increase the loss.

If the security is purchased and sold in Canadian dollars, the capital gain or loss is simply the profit or loss you incurred. If the security is purchased in a foreign currency (a U.S. stock, WEBS, or ADR), the capital gain or loss must be calculated using the Canadian-dollar value of each purchase and sale. If you purchased the foreign stock from a Canadian-dollar account, then your Canadian-dollar purchase and sale values are easily found on the financial statements sent to you by your discount broker. If purchased or sold from a U.S. dollar account, record the exchange rate of the day in your log. Check a newspaper for the exchange rate or ask your discount broker. Be sure to log all stock purchases and sales. If you forget to log the exchange rate, you can call Revenue Canada at tax time for acceptable exchange rates to use.

Any capital gains in a year may be reduced by any capital losses in that year. If it's a net capital gain, 75% of the gain is taxable. If it's a net loss, then 75% of the net capital loss may be applied against the taxable portion of any future capital gain or carried back up to three years to be applied against the taxable portion of a previous capital gain. It's important to keep track of any ongoing net capital loss, so that it may be used in the future to offset future or past capital gains. Make a note of any ongoing net capital loss in your log and in your annual tax return.

> **O**n the tax return, any net capital loss being applied to a current year's capital gain is entered on page three to reduce your taxable income. To carry back a net capital loss, you need to fill out a "Request For Loss Carryback" form. Details about capital gains taxation are contained in the Capital Gains guide. ⊙————

When considering whether to sell a stock, also consider the tax implications of such a move. For example, selling a losing stock as well as part or all of a winning stock in the same year can minimize—or eliminate—capital gains.

THE CHECKUP

Just like going to the dentist, investment portfolio checkups are very important!

There are two kinds of checkups—monthly and annual. The monthly checkup is simple and takes anywhere from two minutes to an hour. The annual checkup is more detailed.

The monthly checkup consists mainly of checking to see if you have enough money to make a purchase of a stock or a bond. Discount brokers usually mail you a statement of your holdings every month, as long as there was some activity in your account (a deposit, trade, dividend, etc). The statement will show you how much cash you have. If there has been no activity and you don't know what your cash balance is, you might have to put a call in. This can be done with automated telephone trading as well.

Agood way to ensure that cash is building up in your investment account or RRSP account is to start a pre-authorized chequing system, which most of the discount brokers offer. Putting aside, say, $100, $200, or 10% of your after-tax income every month is a great way to build up cash to make investments with. Your set amount of cash will be taken from your chequing or savings account each month and deposited into your RRSP or non-RRSP investment account or both in the form of cash.

THE ANNUAL CHECKUP

The annual checkup takes longer than the monthly checkup. This is where you set aside a block of time once a year (or more frequently if you prefer) to go over your entire savings portfolio. Any day of the year will do; just remember to actually do it. If you have any friends who invest on their own, you might find getting together for the checkup is more fun. If you're purely an index stock investor, the annual checkup will probably take less than an hour. For those with individual stocks, it will take longer.

If you own or plan to buy any individual Canadian stocks, make sure to get a recent copy of the *Toronto Stock Exchange Review*. Also buy a copy of *The Globe and Mail* or *The Financial Post*. *The Wall Street Journal* will also come in handy for U.S. and international stocks and WEBS quotes.

Gather up all of your financial statements plus your investment log and set them out on the kitchen table or on the big desk in the study. Turn off the TV and send the kids to the movies.

Note in your log the day of your annual checkup. Also note the level of the TSE 300 index and any other indexes that you are invested in or interested in. Then note the price of all of the index-linked stocks, individual stocks, and mutual funds that you own.

Look over your investments and get a feel for how they've been performing. It's helpful to write a quick blurb about each of your investments—for example, "BigCo Inc. up 15% in past year," or "Live Bait Corp. lower again this year." Past blurbs make for quick analysis at annual checkup time.

When you get into your second and subsequent annual check-ups, compare the current value of each investment with prior years' levels and with the value at the time you made the investment.

WHAT ELSE SHOULD YOU CHECK?

Check to see that your dividend-paying stocks are still paying you dividends. You can find this out by looking at the list of stocks in the blue pages of *The TSE Review*, which includes each company's div-idend yield. The dividend yield is also in the newspapers' stock tables. You can also check the amount of the stock's last quarterly dividend in your statements.

Ask yourself the following questions to see if your portfolio needs to be rebalanced at all to match your investment approach, and to determine if it's time to sell any stocks. Keep in mind your chosen investment approach (such as TIPS with a few dividend stocks, tilted index approach, mostly stocks or all-stock approach). If your portfolio does require rebalancing, then plan to do it soon or as you make any new investments in the coming months.

- Are my Canadian stocks still included in the TSE 300?
- Did any stocks nosedive?
- Do any single individual stocks account for more than 25% of my overall savings?
- Have any stocks trended lower over a few years even as the stock market moved ahead?
- Are my stock investments properly diversified by industry, TSE 300 weighting, and do some pay dividends?
- Does my overall portfolio have a strong international profile?
- Is my breakdown between stocks and bonds appropriate for my age and risk tolerance?
- Do I have any bonds maturing in the next few months?
- Are my bonds diversified by maturity date?
- Have I made my maximum allowable RRSP contribution for this year and kept track of unused room from previous years?

Once you've decided if you need to rebalance, jot in the log what changes should be made for future reference. If you're still saving, you'll probably be able to rebalance as you invest new money. Make a note of any TIPS, Spiders, Diamonds, or WEBS, individual stocks, low-MER international mutual funds, and/or small-cap funds you'd like to buy over the next year.

To help you decide on individual Canadian stocks, open up the *Review* to the green TSE 300 pages and look over stocks that would make good choices for your portfolio. Make sure the new candidates are a good complement to the stocks you already own—in other words, stick to your investment approach and continue to diversify.

Some stocks will be new to the TSE 300 since your last checkup and won't be found in this book's TSE 300 list with accompanying blurbs. The only clue the *TSE Review* gives you about the company's area of business is the industry grouping or sub-group that the stock belongs to. This is probably enough of a guideline to keep your picks diversified by industry. But to find out more about a company you might choose to do some research either through your discount broker, on the Internet, or at the library.

THE MONTHLY CHECKUP

Once a month, check on your financial situation to see if you have enough cash to make a new investment. The easiest time to do this is when you receive your monthly statement, but you can do it whenever you want.

If you only have a couple hundred bucks in loose cash, it's probably too soon to invest it. Your cash will earn some interest while it sits there, but you can almost always get a higher rate if you transfer your loose cash to a money-market mutual fund until you invest it. Money-market funds invest in government treasury bills and other short-term investments that pay interest. If your discount broker account is with one of the banks, sticking with the bank's money-market fund often means that there are no added fees to buy or sell the fund. Just be sure to transfer any money-market fund money into cash if you need it when you do your next trade.

If you do have enough cash to invest, then decide what to invest in. Consult your log's last annual checkup to refresh your memory.

> Remember the rule of thumb about keeping your commissions to 2% or less of the value of your trade. It's okay to go above this figure as long as you have every intention of holding your investment for many years. The 2% rule is aimed at making your investments as cost-effective as possible.

Remember that you can make a buy order any time of day or night with most of the discount brokers, and you don't have to stick to board lots of 100 shares. For example, if you find one month you have $1,362 in cash, and TIPS 100 is trading at $50 per share, you could buy 25 shares of TIPS 100 for $1,250 plus a commission of $25.

Of course, there's no need to panic and buy something every time you have $1,000 in cash saved up. Just don't let several thousand dollars sit in cash for months on end, and keep your idle cash in a money-market fund until you have enough to invest.

SPECIAL SITUATIONS

TAKEOVERS

If you own shares of a company that is the target of a takeover by another company, you will likely be contacted by mail to be apprised of the takeover offer. Don't worry; it doesn't happen very often. Materials sent may include a form or a phone number that allows you to accept the offer and "tender" your shares to the acquiring company. You don't have to respond to any such offer if you don't want to accept it or just don't feel like it. Your shares, however, may be automatically acquired by the acquiring company if 90% of the target company's shareholders agree to the takeover. When one of your companies is taken over, you will receive cash for your shares or a certain number of the acquiring company's shares, or a combination thereof.

> **R**eceiving cash is akin to selling your stock, which means you're on the hook for the capital gain or loss. Receiving shares usually means it's a tax-free deal and you don't need to worry about any capital gain or loss until you sell the shares you received.

STOCK SPLITS

A stock split is when a company decides to reduce the price of its stock. Though the stock's price falls, the stock split has no effect on the amount of money you have invested in the stock. For example, a company whose stock is trading at $90 might decide to split its stock two for one. An investor with 100 shares will now own 200 shares, and the stock will be trading at $45 per share. Stock splits are done mainly to allow smaller investors a better opportunity to buy the stock, since it costs less to buy a board lot.

Sample Portfolios and Final Thoughts

Here are some sample portfolios that incorporate the approaches discussed in this book.

> (f) = RRSP foreign content
> OUT = Outside the RRSP

ALL INDEX AND BONDS PORTFOLIOS

1. $5,000

RRSP $2,500 - 50 shares TIPS 100
        2,500 - Prov. British Columbia 10-year strip bond

A Canadian balanced fund has nothing on this portfolio (except higher fees).

2. $12,000

RRSP $7,000 - 140 shares TIPS 100
         3,000 - Prov. Alberta 10-year strip bond
         2,000 - low MER int'l RRSP index fund

You're talking big diversification in only three long-term investments!

3. $20,000

RRSP $4,500 - 100 shares TIPS 35
         5,000 - 100 shares TIPS 100
         2,500 - Prov. Ontario 10-year strip bond
         2,500 - Prov. Quebec 15-year strip bond
         1,500 - 50 shares WEBS Netherlands (EWN-AMEX) (f)
         2,000 - 100 shares WEBS Mexico (EWW-AMEX) (f)
         2,000 - small-cap mutual fund

Seven investments—big diversification.

4. $40,000

RRSP $14,000 - 300 shares TIPS 100
         5,000 - Prov. Newfoundland 25-year bond
         5,000 - Prov. Alberta 10-year bond
         3,500 - 150 shares WEBS United Kingdom (EWU-
                   AMEX) (f)
         3,500 - 200 shares WEBS Hong Kong (EWH-
                   AMEX) (f)
         4,000 - small-cap mutual fund
OUT   5,000 - 50 shares Spiders mid-cap 400

Big international diversification, and a long-term outside-the-RRSP pick for that sailboat (slightly used) come retirement.

5. $100,000

RRSP $25,000 - 500 shares TIPS 100
         10,000 - 2 different small-cap funds
         10,000 - Prov. Ontario 25-year bond
         10,000 - Prov. Saskatchewan 10-year bond

```
          10,000 - Bell Canada 10-year bond
           5,000 - 200 shares WEBS Germany (EWG-AMEX) (f)
           5,000 - 400 shares WEBS Japan (EWJ-AMEX) (f)
OUT        5,000 - 300 shares WEBS Hong Kong (EWH-AMEX)
           5,000 - 200 shares WEBS Mexico (EWW-AMEX)
          15,000 - 100 shares Spiders S&P 500
```

Index mania! 70% stocks, 30% bonds, and 100% diversification.

Now let's try a few portfolios with some individual stock action.

6. *$19,000*

```
RRSP      $7,000 - 200 shares TIPS 100.
           5,000 - Prov. Ontario 10-year strip bond.
           1,500 - 50 shares TransCanada Pipelines Ltd. (TRP-TSE)
           1,500 - 50 shares TransAlta Corp. (TA-TSE)
           1,000 - 50 shares Mackenzie Financial Corp. (MKF
                    TSE)
           1,500 - 50 shares WEBS France (EWQ-AMEX) (f)
           1,500 - 50 shares WEBS U.K. (EWU-AMEY) (f)
```

The dividends on TRP and TA increase this portfolio's dividend yield while still maintaining good long-term growth potential. Plenty o' diversification.

7. *$35,000*

```
RRSP      $10,000 - 200 shares TIPS 100
            5,000 - Prov. Quebec 10-year bond
            5,000 - Prov. Ontario 25-year bond
            3,000 - 30 shares Microsoft Corp. (MSFT-NASDAQ) (f)
            2,000 - 50 shares Thomson Corp. (TOC-TSE)
            2,000 - 25 shares Dell Computer Corp. (DELL-NAS
                     DAQ) (f)
            5,000 - low MER int'l index RRSP mutual fund
            3,000 - small-cap mutual fund
```

Here's a portfolio with some guts. Three stock picks add some piz-zazz to the TIPS position and reduce the overall exposure to cyclical stocks. Healthy overall diversification. A little extra yield on the Quebec bond as well.

8. *$50,000*

RRSP $10,000 - 200 shares TIPS 100
      10,000 - Prov. Ontario 25-year bond
       5,000 - Prov. B.C. 10-year strip bond
       5,000 - 50 shares Royal Bank of Canada (RY-TSE)
       5,000 - 50 shares Magna International Inc. (MG.A-TSE)
       2,500 - 50 shares Philip Morris Cos. (MO-NYSE) (f)
       2,500 - 25 shares Procter & Gamble (PG-NYSE) (f)
       5,000 - small-cap fund
       2,500 - 100 shares WEBS Switzerland (EWL-AMEX) (f)
       2,500 - 200 shares WEBS Japan (EWJ) (f)

Four stocks in different industries add some zing to the TIPS, and are international companies. The WEBS add more international diversification.

9. *$80,000*

RRSP $10,000 - 200 shares TIPS 100
      10,000 - Prov. Ontario 25-year bond
      10,000 - Prov. Manitoba 10-year bond
       5,000 - 100 shares Bank of Nova Scotia (BNS-TSE)
       5,000 - 100 shares Enbridge Inc. (ENB-TSE)
       5,000 - 100 shares BCE Inc. (BCE-TSE)
       5,000 - 30 shares George Weston Ltd. (WN-TSE)
       5,000 - small-cap fund
       5,000 - 100 shares Power Financial Corp. (PWF-TSE)
       5,000 - RRSP Int'l Index Mutual Fund
       5,000 - 300 shares WEBS Hong Kong (EWH-AMEX) (f)
       5,000 - 200 shares WEBS Netherlands (EWN-AMEX) (f)
       5,000 - 300 shares WEBS Mexico (EWW-AMEX) (f)

Only one word for this portfolio—rockin'! A good balance of index stocks and funds and five different stocks of companies in different industries.

10. $125,000

RRSP	$10,000	-	200 shares TIPS 100 (HIP-TSE)
	10,000	-	Prov. Ontario 25-year strip bond
	10,000	-	Prov. Saskatchewan 10-year strip bond
	10,000	-	Hydro Quebec 15-year bond
	5,000	-	100 shares Canadian Imperial Bank (CM-TSE)
	5,000	-	100 shares Du Pont Canada (DUP.A-TSE)
	5,000	-	30 shares Potash Corp. (POT-TSE)
	5,000	-	100 shares Great West Lifeco Inc. (GWO-TSE)
	5,000	-	100 shares Teleglobe Inc. (TGO-TSE)
	5,000	-	160 shares Loblaw Cos. (L-TSE)
	5,000	-	100 shares Fortis Inc. (FTS-TSE)
	5,000	-	130 shares Maritime T&T (MTT-TSE)
	5,000	-	400 shares WEBS Japan (EWJ-AMEX) (f)
	5,000	-	100 shares PepsiCo. Inc. (PEP-NYSE) (f)
	5,000	-	50 shares Spiders Mid-Cap 400 (MDY-AMEX) (f)
OUT	5,000	-	200 shares WEBS U.K. (EWU)
	5,000	-	100 shares Telefonica de Argentina (TAR-NYSE)
	5,000	-	300 shares WEBS Hong Kong (EWH-AMEX)
	15,000	-	2 small-cap funds

Groovy! Serious diversification and a decent shot at above-average returns.

FINAL THOUGHTS

By golly, we're just about done.

For inexperienced investors, a lot of ground has been covered. While you may not be 100% clear on all the concepts, these will become clearer as you go. I hope the more experienced investors still found the book useful and worth the price of admission.

I hope all readers store a few main points:

- the indexes outperform the mutual funds over the long haul;
- avoiding investment fees and taxes is very advantageous for earning superior long-term returns;
- anyone can invest and pick stocks successfully on his or her own; and
- diversification of investments is crucial.

And even if you decide that do-it-yourself investing isn't for you, I hope you found the book useful as you seek good low-MER funds to buy.

Investors tracking the indexes with TIPS and other index stocks will find it easy to monitor their returns against the mutual funds. Just compare the funds' group averages posted in the newspapers monthly with the relevant benchmark index found either in the newspaper or in the *TSE Review*. Individual-stock investors, however, will find such comparisons more difficult. Calculating precise investment returns is actually a very complicated process that requires number crunching on a home computer. It's a time-consuming, profitless exercise for most. Your monthly financial statements provide plenty of information to give you an idea how your portfolio is doing.

Remember not to get carried away. Some people become obsessed with the market and devote half of their free time to stock-picking. They usually just wind up wasting a lot of valuable time and bore others at parties. Successful do-it-yourself investing can be done in less than an hour a month and a few hours once a year. That leaves more time for the things in life that really matter—like hanging out with the family, reading Hemingway, listening to the Tragically Hip, sitting on a park bench on a crisp November morning, or going to Spain.

Let's face it—only a lucky few ever become fabulously rich simply by picking the right stocks. If getting rich were that easy, we'd *all* be on our private islands in the Caribbean, sipping expensive wines by the pool between chapters in the memoirs. Come to think of it, that kind of life would get boring pretty soon anyway (though it would be nice every February).

So have fun investing on your own. And remember to exercise regularly and eat lots of fruits and vegetables. Healthy body, healthy mind, healthy investment portfolio.

Happy investing.

Appendix

TORONTO STOCK EXCHANGE 300 COMPOSITE INDEX

This list is as of March 1, 1998, and it shows the company's name, the stock symbol, and the stock's weighting in the TSE 300 index. "T35" means the stock is in the Toronto 35 and TIPS 35. "T100" means the stock is in the TSE 100 and TIPS 100. "DIVIDEND" indicates the stock has traditionally paid a solid dividend; and "small DIVIDEND" indicates a smaller dividend. If there's a reference to the company's track record, it generally refers to both the company's earnings performance and stock-price performance.

1.0 METALS & MINERALS (14 STOCKS — 4.78% OVERALL WEIGHT.)

1.1 Integrated Mines

(Big companies that take minerals out of the ground and turn 'em into metal.)

ALCAN ALUMINIUM LTD. (AL), 1.75%, T35, T100.
Makes aluminum, which is used largely in the construction and automotive industries.

COMINCO LTD. (CLT), 0.24%, T100. Zinc, lead, copper, and other base (non-gold) metals.

FALCONBRIDGE LTD. (FL), 0.31%, T100. Makes mainly nickel and copper. A large stake of Falconbridge is owned by Noranda Inc.

INCO LTD. (N), 0.72%, T35, T100. Nickel and copper giant. Nickel is used to make stainless steel for construction and other applications.

NORANDA INC. (NOR), 0.72%, T35, T100, DIVIDEND. Lots of zinc, copper, nickel, aluminum, and magnesium.

SHERRITT INTERNATIONAL CORP. (S), 0.07%. A diversified play on Cuba, including mining, tourism, energy, power, real estate, agriculture, telecommunications, and other ventures on the island nation. Some political risk.

1.2 *Mining*

(Companies that do the mining and milling but let smelters and refiners make the finished metal products. No comment means typical small mining company.)

AUR RESOURCES INC. (AUR), 0.04%. Base metals.

CAMECO CORP. (CCO), 0.42%. Mines uranium, which fuels nuclear reactors. Also mines gold.

BREAKWATER RESOURCES LTD. (BWR), 0.03%.

INTERNATIONAL CURATOR RESOURCES LTD. (IC), less than 0.01%.

INMET MINING CORP. (IMN), 0.09%. Mid-size mining company.

LIONORE MINING INTERNATIONAL LTD. (LIM), 0.02%.

INCO LTD. CLASS VBN (N.V), 0.08%. A pure play on the Voisey's Bay nickel mine in Labrador.

RIO ALGOM LTD. (ROM), 0.28%, T100, DIVIDEND. Copper miner with a metals-distribution division.

2.0 GOLD & PRECIOUS METALS
(36 STOCKS — 5.41% OVERALL WEIGHT.)

(Just like the mining companies, except they mainly mine gold and silver. No comment means typical gold miner.)

BARRICK GOLD CORP. (ABX), 1.79%, T35, T100. Big low-cost gold mining company with extensive mineral reserves and long track record of solid earnings.

ABER RESOURCES LTD., (ABZ), 0.11%. Diamond mining.

AGNICO-EAGLE MINES LTD. (AGE), 0.07%. Gold mining with some base metal mining under development.

BEMA GOLD LTD. (BGO), 0.06%. Gold and copper mining.

BATTLE MOUNTAIN CANADA LTD. (BMC), 0.12%.

CAMBIOR INC. (CBJ), 0.11%.

DAYTON MINING CORP. (DAY), 0.02%.

DIA MET MINERALS LTD. (DMM.B). 0.07% Diamond mining.

ECHO BAY MINES LTD. (ECO). 0.07%. Gold and silver mining.

ELDORADO GOLD CORP. (ELD), 0.01%.

EURO-NEVADA MINING CORP. (EN), 0.36%, T100. Big gold-royalty company and gold producer.

FRANCO-NEVADA MINING CORP. (FN), 0.42%, T100. Sister to Euro-Nevada. Biggold-royalty company, gold producer and growing oil royalties.

GOLDCORP INC. (G.A), 0.08%.

GLAMIS GOLD LTD. (GLG), 0.03%.

GREENSTONE RESOURCES LTD. (GRE), 0.09%.

GOLDEN STAR RESOURCES LTD. (GSC), 0.03%.

INDOCHINA GOLDFIELDS LTD. (ING), 0.02%.

KINROSS GOLD CORP. (K), 0.11%. Mid-size gold producer.

LYTTON MINERALS LTD. (LTL), 0.02%.

MIRAMAR MINING CORP. (MAE), 0.02%.

MERIDIAN GOLD INC. (MNG), 0.06%.

ORVANA MINERALS CORP. (ORV), 0.01%

PAN AMERICAN SILVER CORP. (PAA), 0.06%. Silver mining.

PLACER DOME INC. (PDG), 0.79%, T35, T100. Big gold company, some copper.

PRIME RESOURCES GROUP INC. (PGU), 0.07%.

RIO NARCEA GOLD MINES LTD. (RNG), 0.02%.

ROYAL OAK MINES INC. (RYO), 0.05%.

SOUTHERNERA RESOURCES LTD. (SUF), 0.05%. Diamond mining.

TECK CORP. (TEK.B), 0.33%, T35, T100. Big gold and base metals miner.

TVX GOLD INC. (TVX), 0.15%. Mid-size gold miner.

VICEROY RESOURCE CORP. (VOY), 0.03%.

3.0 OIL & GAS
(53 STOCKS — OVERALL WEIGHTING 12.44%.)

3.1 Integrated Oils

(Big companies that own vast oil reserves, drill for oil, refine the oil, make oil-related products, and own or franchise gas stations.)

IMPERIAL OIL LTD. (IMO), 0.67%, T100, DIVIDEND.

PETRO-CANADA (PCA), 1.25%, T35, T100.

SHELL CANADA LTD. (SHC), 0.27%, T100, DIVIDEND.

SUNCOR ENERGY INC. (SU), 1.01%, T35, T100.

3.2 Oil & Gas Producers

(These guys search for oil and natural gas, extract it, then sell it to refiners. Some are more into natural gas than oil, but the balance often changes. No comment means typical oil and gas producer.)

ABACAN RESOURCE CORP. (ABC), 0.06%.

ALBERTA ENERGY CO. (AEC), 0.68%, T100.

AMBER ENERGY INC. (AMB), 0.16%.

ANDERSON EXPLORATION LTD. (AXL), 0.36%, T100.

BEAU CANADA EXPLORATION LTD. (BAU), 0.36%.

BLUE RANGE RESOURCE CORP. (BBR.A), 0.04%.

BERKLEY PETROLEUM CORP. (BKP), 0.15%.

BARRINGTON PETROLEUM LTD. (BPL), 0.05%.

BAYTEX ENERGY LTD. (BTE.A), 0.08%.

CABRE EXPLORATION LTD. (CBE), 0.05%.

CHIEFTAIN INTERNATIONAL INC. (CID), 0.07%.

CANADIAN NATURAL RESOURCES LTD. (CNQ), 0.49%, T100.

CRESTAR ENERGY INC. (CRS), 0.21%.

CANADIAN OCCIDENTAL PETROLEUM LTD. (CXY), 0.48%, T100.

DENBURY RESOURCES INC. (DNR), 0.05%.

CANADIAN 88 ENERGY CORP. (EEE), 0.09%.

ENCAL ENERGY LTD. (ENL), 0.07%.

GULF CANADA RESOURCES LTD. (GOU), 0.49%, T100.

GULFSTREAM RESOURCES LTD. (GUR), 0.07%.

HURRICANE HYDROCARBONS LTD. (HHL.A), 0.08%.

NORTHSTAR ENERGY CORP. (NEN), 0.12%.

NUMAC ENERGY INC. (NMC), 0.07%.

NEWPORT PETROLEUM CORP. (NPP), 0.08%.

NORTHROCK RESOURCES LTD. (NRK), 0.10%.

PACALTA RESOURCES LTD. (PAZ), 0.10%.

PANCANADIAN PETROLEUM LTD. (PCP), 0.12%.

PINNACLE RESOURCES LTD. (PNN), 0.07%.

POCO PETROLEUMS LTD. (POC), 0.34%, T100.

PARAMOUNT RESOURCES LTD. (POU), 0.07%.

PENN WEST PETROLEUM LTD. (PWT), 0.11%.

RIO ALTO EXPLORATION LTD. (RAX), 0.14%.

REMINGTON ENERGY LTD. (REL), 0.07%.

RENAISSANCE ENERGY LTD. (RES), 0.59%, T35, T100.

RANGER OIL LTD. (RGO), 0.20%, T100.

TALISMAN ENERGY INC. (TLM), 0.81%, T35, T100.

TRI LINK RESOURCES LTD. (TLR), 0.06%.

TARRAGON OIL & GAS LTD. (TN), 0.08%.

ULSTER PETROLEUMS LTD. (ULP), 0.08%.

3.3 *Oil and Gas Services*

(These companies provide drilling and other services for oil and gas exploration companies. Not considered pure resource stocks.)

CANADIAN FRACMASTER LTD. (CFC), 0.14%.

COMPUTALOG LTD. (CHG), 0.04%.

DRECO ENERGY SERVICES LTD. (DEY), 0.09%.

ENERFLEX SYSTEMS LTD. (EFX), 0.10%.

ENSIGN RESOURCE SERVICE GROUP INC. (ESI), 0.08%.

PRECISION DRILLING CORP. (PD), 0.19%.

PRUDENTIAL STEEL LTD. (PTS), 0.08%.

SHAW INDUSTRIES LTD. (SHL.A), 0.09%.

TESCO CORP. (TEO), 0.11%.

4.0 *PAPER & FOREST PRODUCTS* (18 STOCKS — OVERALL WEIGHTING *2.91%.*)

These companies produce forest products such as pulp, paper, and lumber.)

ABITIBI-CONSOLIDATED INC. (A), 0.52%, T35, T100, small DIVIDEND. Big newsprint and paper producer.

ALLIANCE FOREST PRODUCTS INC. (ALP), 0.19%. Newsprint, paper, and lumber.

BOWATER CANADA INC. (BWX), Pulp and paper.

CASCADES INC. (CAS), 0.06%. Paper and packaging.

CANFOR CORP. (CFP) 0.06%, small DIVIDEND. Lumber and pulp.

DOMAN INDUSTRIES LTD. (DOM.B), 0.04%.

DONOHUE INC. (DHC.A), 0.41%, T100, DIVIDEND. Lumber, pulp, newsprint.

DOMTAR INC. (DTC), 0.15%, T100. Lumber, pulp, paper, packaging.

FLETCHER CHALLENGE CANADA LTD. (FCC.A), 0.20%, T100, DIVIDEND. Pulp, newsprint, paper.

HARMAC PACIFIC INC. (HRC), 0.01%.

INTERNATIONAL FOREST PRODUCTS LTD. (IFP.A), 0.03%.

MACMILLAN BLOEDEL LTD. (MB), 0.39%, T35, T100. Lumber, pulp, newsprint.

NORANDA FOREST INC. (NF), 0.07%, DIVIDEND. Panelboard, lumber, paper, pulp.

REPAP ENTERPRISES INC. (RPP), 0.02%.

SLOCAN FOREST PRODUCTS LTD. (SFF), 0.05%. Lumber, newsprint, pulp, panelboard.

ST. LAURENT PAPERBOARD INC. (SPI), 0.14%. Packaging.

TEMBEC INC. (TBC.A), 0.11%. Lumber, pulp, newsprint.

WEST FRASER TIMBER CO. (WFT), 0.11%. Lumber, packaging, pulp.

5.0 CONSUMER PRODUCTS (19 STOCKS — 5.79% OVERALL WEIGHTING.)

5.01 Food Processing

MAPLE LEAF FOODS INC. (MFI), 0.07%. Makes the Maple Leaf brand pork and other meat products, plus bread and baked goods and animal food. An erratic history, but improvements are being made. Owns majority stake in Canada Bread Co. (CBY-TSE), a solid long-term performer.

SASKATCHEWAN WHEAT POOL (SWP.B), 0.11%, small DIVIDEND. Grain processor. Also into canola, flour, barley, and other stuff that makes food.

VAN HOUTTE A.L. Ltee. (VH), 0.09%. Coffee products and cafes.

5.02 Tobacco

IMASCO LTD. (IMS), 1.25%, T35, T100, DIVIDEND. Big diversified consumer products and financial services company. Owns Imperial Tobacco (du Maurier and Players cigarettes), Shoppers Drug Mart and other stores, and Canada Trust. A play on smokes, retail, and financial services. A solid long-term performer.

ROTHMANS INC. (ROC), 0.05%, DIVIDEND. Rothmans and Benson & Hedges cigarettes.

5.03 *Distilleries*

SEAGRAM CO. (VO) 2.13%, T35, T100, small DIVIDEND. World-wide booze giant. Sells liquor under Seagram, Chivas Regal, Absolut, and other brands. Also owns MCA, an entertainment company that produces movies, music, and theme parks, and Polygram, one of the world's biggest recorded music companies.

5.04 *Breweries and Beverages*

COTT CORP. (BCB) 0.10%. Makes most of the private-label soft drinks you get in supermarkets across Canada, the United States, the United Kingdom, and elsewhere. Once a market darling, Cott's been hurt by a long pop price war in recent years. New CEO was named in June 1998.

MOLSON COS. (MOL.A), 0.21%, T100, DIVIDEND. Beer. Canadian, Export, Coors Light, etc. Also owns Beaver Lumber and the Montreal Canadiens. Mainly a beer play.

5.05 *Household Goods*

CCL INDUSTRIES INC. (CCQ.B), 0.10%. Packaging and manufacturing services.

CINRAM INTERNATIONAL INC. (CRW), 0.27%, T100. Compact discs, CD-ROMs, video tapes, audio cassettes, VHS cassettes, etc.

INTERNATIONAL COMFORT PRODUCTS CORP. (ICP), 0.08%. Heating and cooling equipment for homes and businesses.

5.08 *Biotechnology/Pharmaceuticals*

(There are development-stage drug companies, which are very risky, and there are approved drug makers, which are less risky.)

ALLELIX BIOPHARMACEUTICALS INC. (AXB), 0.03%. Developing drugs for osteoporosis and other diseases.

BIOCHEM PHARMA INC. (BCH), 0.61%, T100. Makes and researches anti-disease drugs, including AIDS treatment 3TC.

BIOMIRA INC. (BRA), 0.03%. Developing drugs for cancer.

BIOVAIL CORP. INTERNATIONAL (BVF), 0.22%. Makes/researches drugs for hypertension, arthritis, and obesity.

TLC THE LASER CENTRE INC. (LZR), 0.06%. Laser eye surgery to correct vision.

MDS INC. (MHG.B), 0.24%, T100. Big international health services company that sells laboratory services, hospital supplies, and technological products to treat, diagnose, and prevent disease. MDS's stock has been a solid performer in recent years.

PHOENIX INTERNATIONAL LIFE SCIENCES INC. (PHX), 0.04%. Provides research services for the pharmaceuticals and biotechnology industries.

QLT PHOTOTHERAPEUTICS INC. (QLT), 0.09%. Develops and sells light-activated drugs to treat cancer and blindness for the elderly.

6.0 INDUSTRIAL PRODUCTS (59 STOCKS — 17.21% OVERALL WEIGHTING.)

6.1 Steel

(These five companies make steel for a wide range of construction, automotive, pipeline, and other applications.)

ALGOMA STEEL CORP. (ALG), 0.04%.

CO-STEEL INC. (CEI), 0.11%.

DOFASCO INC. (DFS), 0.38%, T35, T100, DIVIDEND.

IPSCO INC. (IPS), 0.29%, T100. The one steel stock in this group that's been a solid long-term performer.

STELCO INC. (STE.A), 0.23%. A much improved company since nearly going under in the early 1990s.

6.2 *Fabricating & Engineering*

AGRA INC. (AGR), 0.05%. International engineering and construction company.

ATS AUTOMATION TOOLING SYSTEMS INC. (ATA), 0.23%, T100. Makes automated manufacturing and test systems for the automotive, consumer products, computer, and health care industries.

INTERTAPE POLYMER GROUP INC. (ITP), 0.13%. Plastics and paper packaging.

LUMONICS INC. (LUM), 0.05%. Laser-based manufacturing systems.

MILLTRONICS LTD. (MLS), 0.05%. Makes industrial measuring equipment.

RUSSEL METALS INC. (RUS.A), 0.04%. Processes and distributes metal.

SNC-LAVALIN GROUP INC. (SNC), 0.09%, small DIVIDEND. International engineering and construction company.

TOROMONT INDUSTRIES LTD. (TIH), 0.09%. Construction equipment, power systems, refrigeration equipment.

UNICAN SECURITY SYSTEMS LTD. (UCS.B), 0.08%. Makes keys and electronic entry systems. Good long-term track record.

UNITED DOMINION INDUSTRIES LTD. (UDI), 0.29%, T100. Makes engineered products such as pumps, valves, and boilers. A big, diversified industrial company.

WESTAIM CORP. (WED), 0.11%. A mixed bag of technology and engineering products.

YBM MAGNEX INTERNATIONAL INC. (YBM), 0.15%. Magnets. Stock-trading halted by market regulators in early 1998. Company auditors refuse to approve earnings. FBI raids corporate head office, amid news reports about possible ties to organized crime. Bad scene.

6.4 *Transportation Equipment*

BOMBARDIER INC. (BBD.B/BBD.A), 1.43%, T35, T100. The well-known snowmobile (Skidoo) king is also the maker of jets and airplanes (Learjet, DeHavilland etc.), jet skis (Seadoo), subway cars, and more. A diversified transportation/consumer products play.

MAGELLAN AEROSPACE CORP. (MAL), 0.06%. Makes and repairs flight-industry parts and equipment.

WESTERN STAR TRUCK HOLDINGS LTD. (WS), 0.04%. Makes big trucks.

6.5 *Technology — Hardware*

(Technology and software companies come and go with the wind. Long-term investors are best off sticking with the big, established companies like Nortel and Newbridge, or keeping a close eye on any other picks made.)

ATI TECHNOLOGIES INC. (ATY), 0.21%. Makes multimedia and graphics products for computers. Stock has soared in last few years.

CAE INC. (CAE), 0.21%, T100. Makes flight simulators for training. This stock has been a long-term dud.

COM-DEV INTERNATIONAL LTD. (CDV), 0.13%. Makes wireless communications products for satellite-, microwave-, and radio-based communication systems.

C-MAC INDUSTRIES INC. (CMS), 0.08%. Makes electronic components for telecom equipment. Strong performance in recent years.

CANADIAN MARCONI CO. (CMW), 0.04%. Makes electronic communication products.

GENNUM CORP. (GND), 0.06%. Makes silicon circuits.

JDS FITEL INC. (JDS), 0.15%. Makes products for the fibre-optic communications industry. Strong stock performance over the last few years.

LEITCH TECHNOLOGY CORP. (LTV), 0.14%. Makes products to distribute and process video and audio signals.

MOORE CORP. (MCL), 0.34%, T35, T100, DIVIDEND. Business forms, labels, and printing services. Not really a tech stock. Company is trying to restore its former glory.

MITEL CORP. (MLT), 0.34%, T100. Telecom software and hardware supplier with erratic history, but stabilized in recent years.

NEWBRIDGE NETWORKS CORP. (NNC), 0.78%, T100. Big international maker of high-tech communication network products and systems. Volatile, but successful track record.

NORTHERN TELECOM LTD. (NTL), 3.43%, T35, T100. "Nortel" is a telecommunications giant with a presence all over the planet. Makes telecom and networking equipment for the world's major phone companies and telecommunications providers.

RAND A TECHNOLOGY CORP. (RND), 0.07%. Sells mechanical-design automation tools.

SPAR AEROSPACE CORP. (SPZ), 0.03%. Makes products for space, aviation, communications, and defence industries. Laggardly historical stock performance.

SR TELECOM INC. (SRX), 0.03%. Makes products for rural telephone systems.

6.06 *Building Materials*

CFM MAJESTIC INC. (CFM), 0.08%. Makes gas and wood-burning fireplaces.

JANNOCK LTD. (JN), 0.11%, small DIVIDEND. Supplies a range of construction materials.

MAAX INC. (MXA), 0.05%. Bathroom-equipment manufacturing.

PREMDOR INC. (PDI), 0.09%. Makes residential doors.

ROYAL GROUP TECHNOLOGIES LTD. (RYG), 0.30%, T100. Building products, housing, and storage-building systems.

6.07 *Chemicals and Fertilizers*

(There are some solid long-term performers in here. Chemicals and fertilizers may be boring, but there's usually steady demand for these raw materials.)

AGRIUM INC. (AGU), 0.42%, T100. Big fertilizer supplier. Solid performance in recent years.

AT PLASTICS INC. (ATP), 0.03%. Makes specialty plastic products.

CELANESE CANADA INC. (CCL), 0.09%, DIVIDEND. Makes synthetic fibres, textiles, and chemicals. Strong history.

DU PONT CANADA (DUP.A), 0.16%. Chemicals, fibres, plastics. Solid long-term performance.

METHANEX CORP. (MX), 0.27%, T100. Major supplier of methanol (vehicle fuel). Long-term prospects for methanol unclear.

NOVA CORP. (NCX), 1.24%, T35, T100. Plastics and chemicals.

POTASH CORP. (POT), 1.20%, T100. Major international fertilizer supplier. Good past record.

6.10 *Technology — Software*

COREL CORP. (COS), 0.03%. Struggling maker of CorelDraw and WordPerfect software. Competing with Microsoft, the Goliath of the software market.

COGNOS INC. (CSN), 0.28%, T100. Software for data analysis; sells to a broad range of business customers.

DELRINA CORP. (DE), 0.09%. Flashy start in early 1990s with computer screensavers and fax software. Not much action since.

PC DOCS GROUP INTERNATIONAL (DXX), 0.02%. Software for document and data management.

GEAC COMPUTER CORP. (GAC), 0.60%, T100. Provides computer solutions for business and governments. Solid track record.

CGI GROUP INC. (GIB.A), 0.14%. Information technology consulting company.

HUMMINGBIRD COMMUNICATIONS CORP. (HUM), 0.13%. Sells software that allows access to network-based information databases.

6.11 *Autos and Parts*

BALLARD POWER SYSTEMS INC. (BLD), 0.39%, T100. Makes vehicle fuel cells, which convert hydrogen and oxygen into electricity. Stock has soared on expectations, but no earnings yet.

LINAMAR MACHINE CORP. (LNR), 0.36%, T100. A diversified auto-parts supplier with a strong long-term track record in earnings and stock price.

MAGNA INTERNATIONAL INC. (MG.A), 1.05%, T35, T100. One of North America's biggest and most innovative auto-parts suppliers, with extensive operations in North America, Europe, and elsewhere. A premier Canadian company.

7.00 REAL ESTATE
(6 STOCKS — 1.56% OVERALL WEIGHT.)

(A cyclical industry with few long-term winners.)

BROOKFIELD PROPERTIES CORP. (BPC), 0.11 %. Owns and operates office buildings and develops residential property.

CAMBRIDGE SHOPPING CENTRES (CBG), 0.21 %. Owns and operates shopping malls.

GENTRA CORP. (GTA), 0.10 %. Owns various Canadian commercial real-estate properties.

INTRAWEST CORP. (ITW), 0.16 %. Operates resorts including Whistler/Blackcomb in B.C., Mont Tremblant in Quebec.

OXFORD PROPERTIES (OXG), 0.09 %. Owns office and retail properties in Canada.

TRIZECHAHN CORP. (TZH), 0.89 %, T100. Owns office towers and development properties in North America and Europe.

8.00 TRANSPORTATION & ENVIRONMENTAL SERVICES
(7 STOCKS — 3.32% OVERALL WEIGHT.)

AIR CANADA (AC) 0.27 %, T100 (Air Canada Class A (AC.A) 0.08 %). Canada's biggest airline. Erratic history, but company revitalized in recent years.

CANADIAN NATIONAL RAILWAY CO. (CNR), 1.32 %, T35, T100. Just what it says, also with a north-south U.S. route. Solid performance since being privatized a few years ago.

LAIDLAW INC. (LDM), 1.20 % T35, T100. Environmental services; also operates school buses and ambulances.

PHILIP SERVICES CORP. (PHV), 0.31 %, T100. Industrial services company's stock plunged in early 1998 as a major copper-trading scandal surfaced. Future uncertain.

TRIMAC LTD. (TMA), 0.07 %. Trucking and truck leasing.

TRANSAT A.T. INC. (TRZ), 0.07 %. Air Transat charter airline.

9.00 PIPELINES
(3 STOCKS — 2.73% OVERALL WEIGHTING.)

(These companies are a lot like utilities. The stocks pay dividends but still have good long-term growth potential.)

ENBRIDGE INC. (ENB), 0.83%, T100, DIVIDEND. Operates oil pipeline from Canada to the United States and holds stake in other pipeline projects. Also owns Consumers Gas, Canada's biggest natural gas company. A nice two-pronged utility play.

TRANSCANADA PIPELINES LTD. (TRP), 1.24%, T35, T100, DIVIDEND. Major North American natural gas pipeline operator with growing international operations. Took over Nova Corp.'s pipeline assets in mid-1998.

WESTCOAST ENERGY INC. (W), 0.65%, T100, DIVIDEND. Natural gas pipeline operator in Western Canada with international projects.

10.00 UTILITIES
(23 STOCKS — 10.62% OVERALL WEIGHTING)

(This is the land of dividends and—usually—steadily increasing corporate earnings and stock prices. Utilities make up many of the common-share stocks that show up in dividend mutual funds and—usually—make safe, core holdings for a stock portfolio.)

10.01 Telephone Utilities

(Most of Canada's telephone companies have soared in the past few years. Near-term returns are unlikely to match, but these are still good buys for the long term.)

BCE INC. (BCE), 5.62%, T35, T100, DIVIDEND. Canada's biggest telecommunications company. Owns the Bell Canada long-distance and local telephone company, a major stake in Northern Telecom Ltd. and BCE Mobile, plus other international telecommunications businesses. A nicely diversified telecommunications play, and a must-own for the non-TIPS investor seeking to approximate the Canadian stock market.

BC TELECOM INC. (BCT), 0.51%, T100, DIVIDEND. British Columbia's dominant telephone company. Solid long-term track record.

BCE MOBILE COMMUNICATIONS INC. (BCX), 0.16%. Cell-phone company Bell Mobility has dominant share of Quebec/Ontario cell-phone market. A play on wireless phone usage.

BRUNCOR INC. (BRR), 0.10%, DIVIDEND. Owns NBTel, the New Brunswick-based phone company.

CALL-NET ENTERPRISES INC. (CN), 0.08%, CALL-NET ENTER-PRISES class B (CN.B), 0.08%. This is Sprint Canada, which operates long-distance telephone service to businesses and homes; also has an Internet service.

FONOROLA INC. (FON), 0.10%. Operates long-distance telephone service to businesses and homes.

MANITOBA TELECOM SERVICES INC. (MBT), 0.26%, T100, DIVIDEND. Local, long-distance, and cell-phone telephone service provider.

MARITIME TELEPHONE & TELEGRAPH (MTT), 0.12%, DIVIDEND. Local, long-distance, and wireless telephone service provider for Nova Scotia, and to P.E.I. through major stake in Island Telephone Co. (IT-TSE).

NEWTEL ENTERPRISES LTD. (NEL), 0.05%, DIVIDEND. Local, long-distance, and wireless telephone service provider for Newfoundland.

CLEARNET COMMUNICATIONS class A (NET.A), 0.09%. Operates the "Mike" PCS wireless communication service.

QUEBECTEL GROUP INC. (QTG), 0.05%, DIVIDEND. Local, long-distance, and wireless telephone service provider for eastern Quebec.

ROGERS CANTEL MOBILE COMMUNICATIONS class B (RCM.B), 0.04%. Provides wireless communications services nationally, through the Cantel brand.

TELUS CORP. (T), 0.91%, T100, DIVIDEND. Local, long-distance, and wireless telephone service provider for Alberta.

TELEGLOBE INC. (TGO), 0.40%, T100. Unique among the telecom companies—operates overseas telecommunications services for Canadian telcos, and has growing international telecommunications operations.

TELESYSTEM INTERNATIONAL WIRELESS INC. (TIW), 0.30%, T100. Cellular telecommunications service provider in emerging nations such as China and India; wireless communications provider in Europe.

10.04 *Gas/Electrical Utilities*

ATCO LTD. (ACO.X), 0.17%, DIVIDEND. A holding company—owns majority of Canadian utilities and housing division.

BC GAS INC. (BCG), 0.24%. DIVIDEND. Supplies natural gas for British Columbia and operates oil pipeline.

CANADIAN UTILITIES class A (CU), 0.19% (CANADIAN UTILITIES class B (CU.X) (0.06%)), DIVIDEND. Electricity and gas supplier for Alberta, plus other power, water, and natural gas businesses in Canada and abroad.

FORTIS INC. (FTS), 0.10%, DIVIDEND. Electric utility for Newfoundland and P.E.I. plus a mishmash of smaller investments.

NOVA SCOTIA POWER INC. (NSI), 0.29%, T100, DIVIDEND. Electric utility for Nova Scotia.

TRANSALTA CORP. (TA), 0.67%, T35, T100 DIVIDEND. Alberta electric utility, with some international power projects.

11.00 COMMUNICATIONS & MEDIA (18 STOCKS — 3.5% OVERALL WEIGHTING.)

11.01 *Broadcasting*

BATON BROADCASTING INC. (BNB), 0.17%. Owns television stations and a stake in CTV network.

CANWEST GLOBAL COMMUNICATIONS CORP. (CGS.S), 0.21% (CANWEST GLOBAL COMMUNICATIONS CGS.A, 0.07%.) Television broadcaster (Global), with interests in broadcasting in Australia and New Zealand. Solid track record.

CHUM LTD. class B (CHM.B), 0.06%. Television and radio broadcasting. Stock has soared in recent years.

WIC WESTERN INTERNATIONAL COMMUNICATIONS LTD. class B (WIC.B), 0.10%. Television and radio broadcasting. Subject of takeover attempts in spring 1998.

11.02 *Cable and Entertainment*

(Cable companies generally enjoy steady income, and some see value in cable networks as superior to telephone lines for home computer links.)

CINAR FILMS INC. (CIF.B), 0.12%. Programming for kids. This stock trades very little.

IMAX CORP. (IMX), 0.12%. The large-screen movie company.

ROGERS COMMUNICATIONS INC. class B (RCI.B), 0.12%. Biggest television cable operator in Canada. Also owns major stake in Rogers Cantel cell-phone company, radio stations, and Maclean Hunter publishing. Though cable revenue has been solid, this stock has been a poor performer for many years, as losses have piled up amid a mountain of debt.

SHAW COMMUNICATIONS INC. (SCL.B), 0.19%, T100. Major Canadian cable operator, with stakes in a few specialty TV channels and radio stations. Good long-term track record.

LE GROUPE VIDEOTRON LTEE. (VDO), 0.15%. Quebec-based cable operator with other cable interests.

11.03 *Publishing & Printing*

GTC TRANSCONTINENTAL GROUP LTD. (GRT.A), 0.06%. Commercial printing and publishing company. Major flyer printer.

HOLLINGER INC. (HLG.UN), 0.03%, DIVIDEND. Owns newspapers in Canada, the United Kingdom, the United States, and Israel, as well as a major stake in Southam Inc.

QUEBECOR PRINTING INC. (IQI), 0.23%, T100. Major printing company with international operations. Prints magazines, books, catalogues, inserts, etc.

QUEBECOR INC. class B (QBR.B), 0.19%, T100 (class A (QBR.A), 0.05%). Publishes newspapers, books, etc. Owns a major stake in Quebecor Printing.

SOUTHAM INC. (STM), 0.16%. Major Canadian newspaper publisher.

THOMSON CORP. (TOC), 1.22%, T35, T100. Major information services and newspaper publishing company. Growing focus: on-line legal, business, and health information.

TORSTAR CORP. (TS.B), 0.24%, T100. Publishes the *Toronto Star* and owns Harlequin books.

12.00 MERCHANDISING
(18 STOCKS — 3.48% OVERALL WEIGHTING.)

12.01 Wholesale Distributors

ACKTION CORP. (ACK), 0.04%. Leasing, financial services, and real estate.

FINNING INTERNATIONAL INC. (FTT), 0.24%, T100. Sells and finances Caterpillar Inc. (CAT-NYSE) agricultural, construction, and mining machinery and equipment. A back-door play on a major U.S. company.

WESTBURNE INC. (WBI), 0.14%. Distributes supplies for electrical, plumbing, and heating/cooling applications.

12.02 Food Stores

(Rain or shine, booming economy or recession, people gotta buy food.)

EMPIRE CO. (EMP.A), 0.07%. Operates food and drug stores in eastern Canada. Stock has soared in last few years after long flat period.

LOBLAW COS. (L), 0.24%, T100. National supermarket chain. Operates Loblaws, Zehrs, SuperValu, and Fortinos supermarkets among others. Solid long-term track record.

METRO-RICHELIEU INC. (MRU.A), 0.14%. Operates Quebec super-markets under Metro, Marche Richelieu, and Les 5 Saisons names among others.

OSHAWA GROUP LTD. (OSH.A), 0.16%. Food wholesaler to IGA, Knechtel, Food Town, and Bonichoix supermarkets, and operates some IGA, Price Chopper stores, and the Pharma Plus drug-store chain. Flat long-term record.

PROVIGO INC. (PGV), 0.10%. Operates Provigo supermarkets in Quebec, Maxi discount stores, and Loeb supermarkets; runs whole-sale operation. Stock has performed poorly for many years.

GEORGE WESTON LTD. (WN), 0.37%, T100. Major bakery com-pany, dairy processor; owns major stake in Loblaw. Strong record.

12.03 *Department Stores*

(Canadian department stores and specialty stores have a spotty long-term track record. Thanks to the Wal-Mart invasion, the indus-try made some much-needed improvements in the mid-1990s but remains highly competitive today.)

HUDSON'S BAY CO. (HBC), 0.30%, T100. Has come a long way since the fur-trading days. Operates The Bay department stores and Zellers discount stores across Canada.

SEARS CANADA INC. (SCC), 0.19%. Operates Sears department stores and catalogue.

12.05 *Specialty Stores*

CANADIAN TIRE CORP. (CTR.A), 0.47%, T35, T100. The venera-ble Canadian retailer. More than just tires.

DYLEX LTD. (DLX), 0.05%. Owns retail chains, including Bi-Way, Braemar, Fairweather, Thrifty's, and Tip Top Tailors.

12.06 *Hospitality*

COUNSEL CORP. (CXS), 0.08%. Operates a U.S. home health care company and pharmacies.

EXTENDICARE INC. (EXE.A), 0.17%, T100. Nursing homes and home care for the elderly; pharmacy and medical supplies.

FOUR SEASONS HOTEL (FSH), 0.19%. Fancy international hotel chain operator.

LOEWEN GROUP INC. (LWN), 0.45%, T100. Funeral home and cemetery operator in the United States and Canada. Remember the old saying about death and taxes? Here's a play on death.

13.00 FINANCIAL SERVICES
(26 STOCKS — 23.22% OVERALL WEIGHTING.)

13.01 Banks and Trusts

(Here is the single biggest sub-group in the TSE 300. Each of the "Big Five" Canadian banks has broad traditional deposit and lending banking operations, mortgages, securities underwriting and full service/discount brokerage operations, mutual funds, and trust operations. Canadian bank stocks have torn up the race track over the last few years. Repeat performance in near term unlikely, but they're solid long-term picks. At least one bank stock is a must for non-TIPS investors.)

BANK OF MONTREAL (BMO), 3.48%, T35, T100, DIVIDEND. Owns Nesbitt Burns securities, InvestorLine discount brokerage, First Canadian mutual funds, Chicago-based Harris Bank, and part of a Mexican bank. Planning merger with Royal Bank by end of 1998.

BANK OF NOVA SCOTIA (BNS), 3.01%, T35, T100, DIVIDEND. Owns ScotiaMcLeod securities, Scotia Discount Brokerage, Scotia Excelsior mutual funds, and stakes in several Latin American banks and other international banking operations.

CANADIAN IMPERIAL BANK OF COMMERCE (CM), 3.28%, T35, T100, DIVIDEND. Owns CIBC/Wood Gundy securities and Investor's Edge discount brokerage, CIBC mutual funds, CIBC/Oppenheimer securities of the United States, and some insurance lines. Planning merger with TD Bank.

ROYAL BANK OF CANADA (RY), 4.50%, T35, T100, DIVIDEND. The biggest of the Canadian banks. Owns RBC Dominion Securities, Action Direct discount brokerage, Royal mutual funds, and Royal Trust. Planning merger with Bank of Montreal.

TORONTO-DOMINION BANK (TD), 3.13%, T35, T100, DIVIDEND. Owns TD Securities, TD GreenLine discount brokerage, and Green-Line mutual funds; has a strong presence in the discount brokerage business in the U.S. Planning merger with CIBC.

NATIONAL BANK OF CANADA (NA), 0.71%, T35, T100, DIVIDEND. A lot like the Big Five banks, but with a Quebec focus. Owns Levesque Beaubien Geoffrion Inc. securities.

LAURENTIAN BANK OF CANADA (LB), 0.09%, DIVIDEND. Smaller Quebec-based bank.

13.03 *Investment Companies and Funds*

AGF MANAGEMENT (AGF.B), 0.15%. Mutual fund company. Sells AGF and 20/20 mutual funds.

C.I. FUND MANAGEMENT INC. (CIX), 0.07%. Mutual fund company.

DUNDEE BANCORP (DBC.A), 0.13%. Owns a grab bag of assets including Dynamic mutual funds.

FAHNESTOCK VINER HOLDINGS (FHV.A), 0.05%. Stock brokerage.

FIRST MARATHON (FMS.A), 0.08%. Securities firm.

INVESTORS GROUP INC. (IGI), 0.26%, T100. Large mutual fund company.

MACKENZIE FINANCIAL CORP. (MKF), T100. Big mutual fund company. Operates Industrial, IVY, Universal, and STAR funds.

MIDLAND WALWYN INC. (MWI), 12%. Stock brokerage and securities firm.

SCEPTRE INVESTMENT COUNSEL LTD. (SZ.A), 0.07%, DIVIDEND. Mutual fund company.

TRIMARK FINANCIAL CORP. (TMF), 0.23%, T100. Mutual fund company.

13.05 *Insurance*

(These are mostly small specialized insurance companies. Stay tuned for some of the big well-known Canadian insurance companies to list their shares on the TSE eventually.)

E-L FINANCIAL CORP.(ELF), 0.11%. Financial services holding company.

FAIRFAX FINANCIAL HOLDINGS LTD. (FFH), 0.62%, T100. Owns several property and casualty insurance companies.

GREAT WEST LIFECO INC. (GWO), 0.29%, DIVIDEND. Major insurance provider in Canada, with U.S. operations as well.

KINGSWAY FINANCIAL SERVICES INC. (KFS), 0.09%. Mainly insures drivers who don't qualify for standard auto insurance.

QUEENSWAY FINANCIAL HOLDINGS LTD. (QFH), 0.06%. Auto insurance.

13.06 *Financial Management*

NEWCOURT CREDIT GROUP INC. (NCT), 1.58%, T100. A major commercial finance and asset-based lending company. Strong growth in its short life.

POWER FINANCIAL CORP. (PWF), 0.51%, T100, DIVIDEND. Holds major stakes in Investors Group mutual funds and Great-West Lifeco insurance, plus European investment concern Pargesa. Solid long-term track record.

TRILON FINANCIAL CORP. (TFC.A), 0.13%, DIVIDEND. Owns stakes in Royal LePage real estate broker, Gentra real estate holdings, and Trilon Securities investment banking.

14.00 CONGLOMERATES
(4 STOCKS — 4.0% OVERALL WEIGHTING.)

CANADIAN PACIFIC LTD. (CP), 2.42%, T35, T100. Large, old cornerstone of Canadian business. Today holds CP Rail lines, CP Ships, PanCanadian Petroleum (PCP-TSE) oil and gas, and CP Hotels. Good performance in recent years.

EDPERBRASCAN CORP. (EBC.A), 0.68%, DIVIDEND. A holding company with major stakes in Noranda Inc. (NOR-TSE), Trilon (TFC.A-TSE), and power generation.

ONEX CORP. (OCX), 0.21%. An investment company that buys underperforming companies, turns them around, then sells them. Currently into electronics manufacturing, airline food catering, auto parts, and other areas.

POWER CORP. OF CANADA (POW), 0.68%, T100. DIVIDEND. Owns a major stake in Power Financial (PWF-TSE), plus newspapers and radio and television stations; has investments in China.

Index